Sue Hoyt

Here's what other marketing gurus are saying about *Confessions of Shameless Self Promoters*™:

"In my 15 years of selling automobiles, I have used many of the marketing techniques that are in this book. I used them so well it got me into the Guinness Book of Records as the World's Greatest Salesperson and inducted into the Automotive Hall of Fame. If you want to do better at marketing yourself, I highly recommend reading this book, it is filled with great marketing techniques!"

> —Joe Girard, author of these world-wide bestsellers: *How to Sell Yourself, Mastering Your Way to the Top. How to Sell Anything to Anybody and How to Close Every Sale.*

Debbie Allen is too modest with the title of her book, which should be, Confessions of Shameless, Sensible, Successful and Solid Self-Promoters. Every page offers enlightenment, served up with warmth and humanity. The lessons she imparts should be mandatory education for entrepreneurs. I give Debbie a shameless and enthusiastic high five!

> —Jay Conrad Levinson, author of *Guerrilla Marketing*™ series of books

I wanted to contribute to this book because I think everybody that has something they love and are passionate about should be a shameless self promoter. I have been a shameless self promoter in everything I believe in. If you are ready to be a superstar you need to be a superstar self promoter. To be leading edge you must be shameless. This book will show you how!

> —Mark Victor Hansen, co-author and creator of *Chicken Soup for the Soul*®

Five stars for Confessions of Shameless Self Promoters! *Debbie Allen did us all a big favor...she collected fascinating stories that not only entertain, but also provide great insight and know how so you too can be a shameless promoter!*

> —Raleigh Pinskey, author of *101 Ways To Promote Yourself and 101 Ways to Promote Your Book Online*

Confessions of Shameless Self Promoters *is definitely the Self Promoters Bible! What an incredible gathering of creative ideas! Hundreds of marketing secrets shamelessly shared. A must-read!*

> —Larry James, professional speaker and author of *How to Really Love the One You're With*

Confessions is a great book—as one who thrives on making Positive Connections®, I was proud to join the ranks of other shameless self promoters. If you don't buy and read this book, shame on you!
   —Deb Haggerty, author of three books, *The Sales Coach, The Communications Coach,* and the *Masters Collection*

Debbie turns great ideas into action when it comes to "Shamelessly" promoting oneself! This is a must read for entrepreneurs serious about increasing their business, and offers advice and ideas from the world's experts in self promotion!
   —Craig Campana, contributing author of *Masters of Networking* and author of *Turning Career Adversity Into Power For Success*

Packed with savvy marketing tips!
   —Randy Gage, author of *How to Build a Multi-Level Money Machine*

Anyone who wants to be somebody and get somewhere in life should read this book, which is full of great ideas! It makes me proud to be a shameless self promoter.
   —Stuart Anderson, Founder,
   Black Angus/Cattle Company Restaurants

When Debbie Allen asked me to pen an essay for her new book, I was flattered. After all, Debbie is a widely recognized, successful marketing guru.
   —Gwen Walters, author of *The Great Ranch Cookbook*

This book is anything but shameless. We don't live on Little House *on the* Prairie *anymore and* Confessions of Shameless Self Promoters *is a must read for anyone who wants to build their business in today's business environment.*
   —Ivan R. Misner, Ph.D.; Founder of BNI,
   Co-author and creator of the bestseller, *Masters of Networking*

Confessions
of
Shameless
Self Promoters™

Confessions
of
Shameless
Self Promoters™

68 Marketing Gurus Share Secrets, Strategies and Unique
Ideas That Will Take You to the Next Level of Success!

By Debbie Allen

Success Showcase Publishing

Printed in the United States of America.

ISBN 0-9650965-5-6

Cartoons featured in this book by Bradford Veley; Marquette, MI
Phone: 906-226-3229 or email: bradveley@aol.com
Cover design: Jim Weems, Ad Graphics
Phone: 800-368-6196 www.thebookproducer.com
Cover photo featured by Jim V. DeLion Photographic Images, Phoenix, AZ
Phone: 602-864-9145 or email: jdelion@mindspring.com
Interior design: The Printed Page, Phoenix, AZ
Phone: 480-460-1707 www.theprintedpage.com
Book Consultant/Editor: Karla Olson, Via Press
Phone: 602-957-1955 or email: viapress@aol.com

Publisher's Cataloging-in-Publication

Allen, Debbie, 1953-
    Confessions of shameless self promoters : 68
marketing gurus share secrets, strategies and unique
ideas that will take you to the next level of success! /
Debbie Allen. -- 1st ed.
    p. cm.
    Includes index.
    ISBN: 0-9650965-5-6

    1. Marketing. I. Title.

HF415.A45 2001   658.8
                    QBI01-200318

Debbie Allen, of "self-promotion fame," is an international professional speaker, author, and business consultant. As a business owner and entrepreneur for over two decades, Debbie's acute business sense and thirst of knowledge is teamed with her enthusiasm for business marketing to mean great success.

Starting out in a family car rental and mini-storage business right out of high school, Debbie learned hands-on business from the school of hard knocks. After 14 years, Debbie sold her shares of the family business and purchased her first retail apparel store. With no retail background yet a keen business sense, within a few years Debbie grew this struggling store over 10 times to $2 million annually. She continued to build and then successfully sell two additional retail stores.

With expertise in business marketing and the retail industry, Debbie now shares her knowledge and passion, teaching audiences how to out- market, out-sell, and out-profit their competition. Topics include: "Shamelessly Successful Self Promotion," "Retail Business Topics," "Visual and Promotional Marketing," "Internet Marketing," "21st Century Customer Service," "Sales Training for the New Economy," "The Science of Sales," and "Diversified Selling to Different Generations and Genders."

Debbie is the author of two books on business marketing, *Trade Secrets of Retail Stars* and *Confessions of Shameless Self Promoters*. Debbie is the editor of two online newsletters and is also a freelance writer for numerous national trade publications. Debbie is the presenter and producer of a 12-part tele-seminar series, "How to Out-Market, Out-Sell, and Out-Profit the Competition." She also has a sales training system, "Creating Your Dream Team."

Debbie received the 1997 Blue Chip Enterprise Award, sponsored by the National Chamber of Commerce. She served as president for National Speakers Association Arizona Chapter from 1999 to 2000. In addition, she is the founder of Self Promotion Month (October) and International Business Image Improvement Month (May), both featured in *Chase's International Book of Special Events* and *Celebrate Today*.

Acknowledgments

This exciting book would not exist without my wonderfully successful contributors. My deepest appreciation goes out to all of them. Thank you for allowing me to hear your most secret and shameless confessions of self promotion and to share them with the world.

Thank you for generously sharing your confessions. Your confessions of successful marketing strategies, unique and humorous events, along with your secrets from failure to success, will inspire everyone who reads this book.

A truly successful person is one who understands about giving back. The successful entrepreneurs, speakers, and authors included in this book understand the meaning of this. They have had the opportunity to learn from others and now are in a position to share their own personal failures and business successes with you to help you grow and prosper as well.

In addition, I would like to thank everyone that helped make this book come together so successfully and painlessly. A special thanks goes out to my book consultant and editor, Karla Olson from Via Press. You kept me on track every step of the way and challenged me to learn and improve in the process. Another special thank you goes out to my book designer, Lisa Liddy from The Printed Page. Your attention to detail and your ability to switch gears quickly in mid-process helped to make this book possible.

Last, but certainly not least, I would like to express my deepest appreciation for having the best parents on earth. What a great experience it was to grow up in a family of entrepreneurs who shared their knowledge and advice daily. They taught me to always believe in my career and trust myself. They taught me the importance of being fair and honest in all aspects of my life. And, along the way, though they didn't know it, they were teaching me how to be a shameless self promoter.

Introduction

This collection of shameless marketing concepts, unique ideas, and marketing strategies comes from well-known authors, professional speakers, and successful entrepreneurs. Through all the contributions runs a common thread: a true belief that self promotion has helped them to rise above their competition, time and time again.

The purpose of this book is to provide you with tips, tools, and ideas to help you market and promote yourself and your business to another level of success. Whether you feel comfortable marketing yourself or not, this book will help you to understand why shameless self promotion is a must to be highly successful today. Shameless simply means having a strong belief in yourself, your services, your products, and what you have to share with the world.

There is no other marketing book quite like this. You will discover the secrets to shameless self promotion and how it will dramatically increase your business with easily implemented ideas. Confessions will jumpstart your brain with tons of creative ideas on how to successfully self promote. The stories will make you laugh along the way.

The contributing authors not only shared their marketing secrets, they confessed to me their deepest, darkest marketing failures and turn-around success stories as well. You will discover some of the best, proven, incredibly successful and gutsy self promotional marketing ideas on:

- ▼ The science of self promotion, why and how it works
- ▼ Building a strong referral base of shameless fans
- ▼ Giving away your service or products to create more business
- ▼ Networking skills and strategies to showcase your expertise
- ▼ Branding your identity and business, why this is crucial in today's marketplace
- ▼ Unique direct mail strategies to make you stand out from the crowd

▼ Cutting-edge Internet marketing secrets to expose your business to the world

▼ Getting tons of media attention to lead you to shameless stardom

▼ Why you should write a book for self promotion and how to market it

▼ Fun stories

▼ And much more!

I hope you enjoy reading this book as much as I have enjoyed creating it. If you learn from this book—and you will!—tell your friends, family, strategic alliances, and business associates about it so they can learn and enjoy the confessions of success as well. But, don't tell your competition. You want to be shamelessly out-marketing them in no time!

Contents

Chapter One

An Introduction to Shameless Self Promotion

If you don't blow your own horn someone else will use it as a spittoon.

—Anonymous

Shameless Self Promotion Step 1: Develop a Strong Belief System

Debbie Allen

When a friend of mine, Larry James, first stated, "I'm a shameless self promoter," I laughed. Then I thought for a moment, and I realized that I'm a shameless self promoter, too. I had never thought of my marketing approach as being shameless before. I would have described myself more like the Energizer Bunny. I just keep on marketing and marketing and doing whatever it takes to make it happen. I had never thought of this as shameful, unless it's shameful to believe in something so much that you want to tell everyone you meet. I call it good marketing!

Growing up in a family of entrepreneurs, I learned early that you must self promote on a daily basis if you want your business to succeed. Since my family had many different businesses, we were always promoting something new. Most of our businesses started out with little or no investment, therefore self promotion was essential to getting those businesses from idea to success.

My father taught me that the first step in marketing success is to have a strong belief in yourself and your ideas. No matter how crazy other people may think your ideas are, you must believe strongly enough to never give up.

Back in the mid-seventies, Dad was on one of his long solo motorcycle trips from Indiana to Texas. While in Texas, he saw a mini-storage facility, one of the first in the nation. The business intrigued him, so he pulled in to inquire. Dad asked the owner detailed questions about the business. The owner was very proud of his new business and open to sharing as he gave him a tour of the grounds. As Dad rode back from Texas, he brainstormed about how he could start his own mini-storage business.

Inspired by his new-found idea, Dad shared the news with the family. Not knowing much about it, we went along with his idea. He had a way of convincing and motivating most anyone when it came to a new business concept. The next step was to go to the bank and get a loan. Simple enough, especially since Dad had proven himself with numerous other business ideas. However, the bank didn't go for it. "I've never heard of a mini-storage business. It sounds like a fad to me. I don't think it will work," said the banker.

Bank after bank turned Dad down, until one banker gave him a small loan based on his past successes. Dad took the small loan and made the rest happen by working long hours on the building's construction. My dad and brother were "hands on" throughout the process, pouring concrete and helping the construction crew finish the project. They turned Dad's new business dream into a reality.

Even before the mini-storage buildings were completed, we had a long list of interested customers. This new fad took off like some crazy dream. As soon as the buildings were completed, they were filled. Before each new building was complete the customer waiting list was full. Finally, the bank believed in the concept. Dad had no problem getting funds to complete a second location. A number of years later, Dad sold the whole operation for a big profit to a major corporation called Public Storage. From start to finish, dad believed in his idea and kept going and going to make it happen. I wonder where I got my determination?

How can you be successful if you don't believe in yourself and what you have to offer to your customers? You can't! Therefore the first step in shameless self promotion is to have a strong belief system. In this chapter you will learn how to discover the beliefs and science behind self promotion. In addition, you will begin to understand how such a belief system will play a strong role in your own success.

The Science of Self Promotion
Jeffrie Story

The first time I heard the words "shameless self promotion" side-by-side with the word "success." I was appalled. How egocentric! How demeaning! Do you mean that, in order to be successful, I have to lower myself to groveling and begging and bragging? Now I know differently. And my new understanding is based on research—not mine, but two behavioral scientists (for whom I am a licensee) named George Dudley and Shannon Goodson, who've made a career out of studying the science of self promotion.

Dudley and Goodson have developed an assessment tool called SPQ*GOLD® and a Fear-Free Prospecting and Self Promotion Workshop®. This assessment identifies ways in which we un-consciously avoid self promotion and limit our success. In nearly 1,000 formal scientific research studies, Dudley and Goodson have found that self promotion is directly related to success.

What have I learned from them? I've learned that, yes, all successful people are self promoters, from Madonna, to Dennis Rodman, to Billy Graham, to Jimmy Carter, to Martin Luther King. Some do it with more political acumen or integrity than others, but we all must self promote to succeed. In fact, we were self promoting in grade school, when we raised our hands in fervor to show the teacher we knew the answer.

Undeniably, there is unethical self promotion. We've all witnessed it, and maybe even lost business to it. But that's not what we're discussing. You can do shameless self promoting with class, ethics, and truth. As Will Rogers said, "If you done it, it ain't braggin."

You'd think I would have known this from my 25 plus years in sales and marketing, but no, I'm still learning. What I want to share with you are the findings from Dudley and Goodson's research, as well as examples of how this might apply to you, and how it fits into your sales and marketing.

Since you're reading this book, you must want to get more business and more clients. And that involves more than those dreadful words, "shameless self promotion." It really involves *making the sale*, which in turn involves tasteful self promotion. A vicious, but symbiotic and exciting, cycle.

Dudley and Goodson, through extensive research, found that there are three behaviors we can learn from natural self promoters. Natural self promoters are those people who don't hesitate to show the world what they can do and have done, and for which they receive recognition in the form of money, fame, or service to others—their *rewards for many* sales. We can emulate what works for them, regardless of our goals.

The first is: **Position.** They position themselves frequently with people who can make a difference in their goals. They automatically wake up each morning asking themselves, "Who can I meet today who will make a difference in my success?" Then they get themselves in front of those people.

Ask yourself the same questions: Who can help me meet my goals? Is it a prospective customer? Is it a colleague who has contacts? Is it an association with key members who may be prospects?

Too frequently we settle for working with the people who are the easiest to reach, not the most *effective*. Work on meeting the *one* person who can have impact on your life, versus the 25 who cannot.

The second behavior of natural self promoters is: **Style.** In marketing, we call this "differentiation." Ask yourself what is it about you that's different, and what makes you *memorable* to your customers or potential clients?

For me, it is frequently my name. How many women do you know named Jeffrie? That doesn't mean that my name will get me places I want to go, but it does mean that when I get there, they remember me more easily. You *must* be remembered!

How do people remember you? Are you distinctive in some way, and do you point it out? If you meet a lot of people and they seem to forget meeting you, you have a problem, but also an opportunity—an opportunity to present yourself in a more *memorable* way. It might be your message, your picture, your business card, your words, your hairstyle. Maybe it's the uniqueness of what you offer, or how you relate your experience to their particular issue, or how you know what their issues are in the first place, or even your personality on the phone! Best of all, it might be your obvious *caring* about them and how you demonstrate that caring.

The third attribute of natural self promoters is: **Repetition**. Natural self promoters don't say it once; they say it many times. If you had seen a wonderful commercial once, would you remember it? Probably not. Advertisers know this principle, which is why they design multiple 'impressions' for their target market, and why we get to see those commercials over and over and over. We, too, have to make multiple impressions in order to achieve "brand awareness."

Repetition also applies to positioning. Once you've found people who can make a difference in your success, find hundreds more!

One lesson I've learned repeatedly is the importance of follow-up calls. Follow up on *everything*—your service, your commitments, your attention to detail, and your mailings. Even follow-up on your follow-up!

In these days of work inundation and multiple priorities, most people don't return phone calls. What does that mean? *Nothing*! Just because you've left them a message doesn't mean you can sit back and wait for a return call. If that's your strategy, you'll lose the business. Keep calling and following up! Keep up the repetition! If it's an existing customer, find reasons to call, such as giving them results of your previous work with them, providing purchasing ideas for the future, etc.

Do the words "shameless self promotion" still grate on you, as they did on me? If so, remember this: You're self promoting because you care about your clients and your potential clients. People want an expert! They *want* anything that can help them meet their goals. That means they want to do business with you. But unless you self promote, they won't know it. If you don't do it, someone else will. How much do you care about your potential customers? If you truly care, let them know through self promotion! Guess what? You both win!

> Jeffrie Story, CSE, has 25 years of successful leadership experience as a director in sales and marketing at a Fortune 500 company. She currently works with corporate sales groups, increasing sales through better use of self promotion, prospecting, account management, and market penetration. You can reach Jeffrie at 480-367-8887 or on the Web at www.Jeffrie.com.

Contrarian Success Strategy

Dan S. Kennedy

The word "shameless" is instructive in and of itself. I am the CEO of the Psycho-Cybernetics Foundation and co-author of a groundbreaking research and writing on the subject of self-image psychology. In my findings I have discovered that many people are held back from properly and fully promoting themselves by limiting instructions and admonitions deeply engraved in their self-images—in essence, matching shame with self promotion.

You cannot afford to be humble. If you wait to be discovered and rewarded based on merit alone, you had better bring a lunch and several good books because you're going to be waiting a long, long time. The bigger your ambitions, the more likely you are to offend people while achieving those ambitions. And your opportunity to have meaningful impact will be in direct proportion to your willingness to offend. What others perceive as arrogance may very well be the level of confidence, self promotion, and pushiness necessary. Also, arrogance magnetically attracts more than it

**"He didn't have a mean bone in his body.
Gosh, I love that in a business competitor!"**

repels because many people prefer association with an individual who is absolutely certain of himself and his convictions.

(Excerpted from *No Rules: 21 Giant Lies about Success*)

> Dan S. Kennedy is a direct-marketing consultant. As a highly recognized professional speaker, he addresses over 200,000 people each year, sharing the platform with others such as President George Bush Sr., General Norman Schwarzkopf, Colin Powell, and Zig Ziglar. Dan is the author of *How to Make Millions with Your Ideas* and *No Rules: 21 Giant Lies about Success*. You can reach Dan at 602-997-7707 or view his website at www.DanKennedy.com.

Shamelessly Making a Difference in People's Lives

Mark Victor Hansen

I wanted to contribute to this book because I think everybody that has something they love and are passionate about should be a shameless self promoter. I have been a shameless self promoter in everything I believe in. Ninety-nine percent of the time it works, and the other one percent gets me in trouble. Most people get scared about the few times it doesn't work. If you get wound up tight about the few things that don't work, it will hold you back to do all the rest that does work.

Am I shameless? Yes! I'm pushing a level of the envelope that no one else has ever thought of pushing. What are you going to do as a statement to make a difference? Most people are not trading what they do for a living at a high enough level. Sure you must first start out with a great product or service to sell. But even then, 90 percent of time you need to spend on that product or service needs to be in marketing and hustling to make it happen.

Jack Canfield and I spent three years putting together *Chicken Soup for the Soul*™. Then we traveled to New York with an agent. We were excited to get the book we believed in so much published. After 33 publishers kicked us out, our agent sent us a letter that stated, "Sorry, but this book is not going to sell." But we never gave up. We then headed to the American Booksellers Association meeting in Anaheim, California (now called Book Expo of America or BEA) with backpacks full of manuscripts. We were turned down by another 134 publishers.

Finally, one little publisher read it, cried all over his silk shirt, and called us in to discuss the book. He stated he would buy it only if we would see to it that we sold 20,000 books ourselves at $6.00 each. The publisher had no risk investing in our book, so we agreed. We asked 100 friends to buy and sell 100 copies each. We busted our bums doing at least five things a day to promote the book and make it happen. Within 18 months we got onto the *New York Times* bestseller list (the list that matters). But even the *New York Times* had to be sold on the concept. They had to be convinced to put our book on the list because of its multiple authors, a concept they did not previously believe in. My comment to that was, "The Bible has 66 authors, just like ours. So you should believe in this book." That got them and they gave in.

By the end of 2000 we will have 37 bestsellers in a row. That's pretty powerful! We've sold 68 million copies, and our goal is to sell one billion copies by 2020, more than any self-help book series in history. No one has ever had 8 best-selling books within one year, except us.

What this book story proves is that we are all born with an infinite capacity. Yet most of us under use it, including myself. If you would have asked me if Jack and I could have pulled all this stuff off I would have told you "no" just five years ago. Instead, we have managed to stay afloat and continually come up with new ideas. Jack and I are always brainstorming, masterminding and encouraging one another.

It takes a lot of energy to take a book on all by yourself. They go in and out of bookstores so fast these days. The publishing industry has gotten tougher, ruder, and harder. In fact, the whole industry lies. It says that you can do a 10 to 20 city book tour and you will have a bestseller. Well, that may happen if your lucky, but it will only last for a week or so. We did not want a flash in the pan, we wanted to get out there and stay out there. By branding our books it has constantly kept us in the public eye.

There are 37 titles in the *Chicken Soup for the Soul*™ series. Most people say that we have peaked already but I certainly don't believe that. I know we have much more *Soup* to go. We continually touch lives and make a difference everyday at a very big level. When someone gives you one of these books it's because they really love you. For example, *Chicken Soup for the Teenage Soul*™ helps young people deal with pain and anguish over these troubled times. Other books touch people who are ill, lose their jobs, or have troubled relationships. Our books give people hope and courage to go forward. Look, the world is in trouble and we feel good about making a difference!

Mark Victor Hansen, Certified Speaking Professional, is co-creator of the Chicken Soup for the Soul™ series. This series has sold more self-help books than any other in history, 68 million copies. Mark presents high-energy, entertaining programs in the area of business motivation and sales. Mark's office may be contacted at 800-433-2314 or view his website to download one of his books for free at www.MarkVictorHansen.com.

Ten Power Principles of Shameless Self Promotion

Don Taylor

When Debbie Allen first proposed the concept of this book, and asked if I would contribute to it, I was nearly insulted. My first thought was: "What would a nice guy like me be doing in a book like that? I'm not a shameless self promoter."

Then upon reflection, I changed my mind. I considered the lives and careers of people I admire. They have this one thing in common: They have confidence in their skills and abilities, and they promote their strengths consistently, subtly, and professionally.

Then I considered my own career. Co-authoring the business bestseller, *Up Against the Wal-Marts* gave me both confidence and a national platform for promotion. Because that promotion was done professionally, I am not ashamed of it. So, I guess that makes me a shameless self promoter after all. Now that I've confessed, I feel better.

So here I will share a condensed version of what I've learned in three careers that span 35 years of success. These concepts have expanded my opportunities and vastly increased my earning power.

Power Principle 1: Understand the Goal

The goal of promotion is to get the right message to the right people at the right time. These three "rights" are critical to your ultimate promotion success.

The right message will give your targeted, first-choice (TFC) customers compelling reasons—advantages and benefits—for doing business with you. Your message must give these customers all the information they need to take the action you desire.

The right person is your TFC customer. Let me elaborate on some elements to look for in your TFC customers. A TFC customer has a serious need or want for what you are promoting. They have the ability to pay full price. They influence others in a positive manner. Once you identify your TFC customers, you can aim your message directly at them.

The right time for promotion leads the need. You should promote prior to the time when your TFC customers are most likely to buy. When will they have a need? Is there a season for what you're promoting and selling? When will your TFC customers be flush with funds?

Power Principle 2: Sell the Truth

Promotion that works in the long term is nothing more than truth well told. In promoting yourself, there is no room for exaggeration, half-truths, and hyperbole.

No promotion based on integrity can be better than the product. Therefore, it is critical to improve the product (you) constantly. You must grow your skills, increase your knowledge, and multiply your talents. New abilities make you worth more and give you new confidence.

Don't try to sell more than you can deliver. Be honest and know your limits.

Power Principle 3: Sweat the Small Stuff

One of the common factors found in the lives of truly successful people is that they are willing to do the things that most people overlook or are too lazy to do. Henry Ford said, "Paying attention to simple little things that most men neglect makes a few men rich."

Small details often fall into four categories: direct promises, implied promises, accuracy, and completeness. It takes time and effort to get the small stuff right. However, the payoff is loyal customers and increased earning power.

The solution is simple: Under-promise, over-deliver. Get it right, get it done.

Power Principle 4: You Live Well by Promoting Your Strengths

Think of those people whose achievements you admire. What do they sell? A physician sells medical knowledge. An artist sells visual pleasure. An accountant sells accuracy and lower taxes. A consultant sells solutions to problems. They live well by selling their strengths.

If your goal is to improve your business, career, or earning power, here is an assignment for you. Make a list of your strengths. Think of the advantages and benefits you can provide others that they can't get from anyone else. Then promote those strengths wholeheartedly.

Power Principle 5: Everywhere You Go, Sell Everything You've Got

Never miss an opportunity to promote everything you've got. I learned this principle from a corporate CEO who began his working career in sales. His company produced several lines. He was calling on a customer who only bought one line. He casually mentioned some other products even though he knew the purchasing agent would have no interest.

However, the purchasing agent was interested, not for his company, but for a friend who was desperately seeking a supplier. He got the referral, and the resultant sale was the biggest of his young career.

Power Principle 6: Promote the Value, Not the Price

Wal-Mart promotes price. Even their trucks are emblazoned with "We sell for less. Always!" Priceline.com is all about price. Their entire website is devoted to inexpensive services.

However, the majority of customers are not price buyers. If all customers were price buyers there would be no Rolex watches, only Timex watches. No T-bone steaks, only bologna. No Lincolns, only Geos.

What all customers want is value. Value is the relationship between price and quality and quantity. Value is a seesaw. Price is on one end of the seesaw, and quality and quantity are on the other. When the customer feels there is a balance, they buy.

Your job as a shameless self promoter is to create value. If you can increase the perception of value, you are worth more. The more you are worth, the more you'll get paid.

Power Principle 7: Forget the Sizzle—Promote the Steak

While I understand the concept of "sell the sizzle, not the steak," I don't agree with it. The steak is tangible. The sizzle is intangible. The steak has substantive qualities like flavor, texture, size, smell, and tenderness. The sizzle is gone as soon as the steak comes off the grill.

Focus on substance. Promote quality. Extol the advantages and benefits you offer. These are lasting, measurable elements. Outlandish gimmicks and schemes are fleeting, marginal promotion techniques.

Hot sizzle will sell a tough steak, but only once. A great steak cooked to perfection will guarantee repeat business. Give your customers great results and they will guarantee your success.

Power Principle 8: Learn the Promotion Power Phrase

Too many would-be promoters use the wrong inducement. They try to sell features, facts, and statistics. People don't buy characteristics, qualities, and numbers; they buy the benefits those elements bring. Therefore, every promotion and every sales pitch should include the power phrase.

The power phrase is, "The benefits to you are…" Put yourself into the customer's place and list the advantages you offer. Then promote the benefits. Even when the benefits seem obvious, point them out.

Power Principle 9: Promote to Elephants

When it comes to potential, all customers are not created equal. If the goal of shameless self promotion is to catapult your career or build your business, promote to the "elephants." These elephants are bigger potential customers that can generate rising revenues and pleasant profits with the lowest possible promotion costs.

Power Principle 10: Move the Cheese

One of the top-selling business books of all time is *Who Moved My Cheese?* by Spencer Johnson, M.D. It is a clever little book about dealing with change.

In the book, four little characters move through a maze in search of cheese. When they find it, they settle in and enjoy their good fortune. Then one day someone moves the cheese. The rest of the book deals with the search for the new cheese.

After reading the book, I realized that if someone was going to be in charge of moving the cheese, I wanted to be that someone. I choose not to be a cheese finder, whose existence depends on finding the cheese. I want to decide where the cheese should go.

The moral of this principle is: Change happens. You can watch it happen and then react to the change, or you can make it happen and let others react.

I choose to be proactive and make change happen. I'll not only move the cheese, but I'll also redesign the maze. Then with a little shameless, but professional self promotion I'll attract a crowd to my maze. I'll help everyone find some cheese. As I help them become successful, they will make me successful.

That's my future. How about yours? Are you going to use these ten power principles to boost your career and increase your earning power? Or will you go on to the next story and let another year slip by while other shameless self promoters achieve their dreams? It's your choice.

We have a saying in Texas that is appropriate at this point. It is, "Wherever you ride to, that's where you are." And so it is with you. The steps you take today will be your destiny tomorrow. I wish you joy and success on your journey.

You Can't Beat Self Promotion

I built a better mousetrap.
It was so very fine,
I knew everyone would want one,
and the market would be mine.

My trap was eco-friendly,
and had benefits galore.
So I watched with baited breath,
for the world to find my door.

But alas, no path was beaten.
The buyers never came.
They knew not of my mousetrap,
and they did not know my name.

They knew not of its quality,
its benefits or price.
They didn't know I'd guarantee
to rid their house of mice.

If you don't wish to sit alone,
in your field of dreams,
I'd recommend some action,
for to me, here's how it seems:

If you want to sell a mousetrap,
you must tell the world about it.
You must advertise and merchandise,
and from the rooftops shout it.

I'd display it in the paper,
I'd send out lots of mail.
I'd show a list of benefits
to help me make the sale.

I'd flash it on my website,
I'd use radio and more,
I'd talk about it everywhere,
and watch my profits soar.

Don't expect the world to find you,
that's what I would advise.
If you want to sell a mousetrap,
it still pays to advertise.

But, you say, I do not have
a single trap to sell.
It's me I want to market,
not a mousetrap or a bell.

I want to sell my talents,
my abilities and skills.
I need to get a good price too,
so I can pay my bills.

So you want to sell yourself, you say
I understand, my friend.
I think I have the answer,
here's what I'd recommend.

You do not need an agent,
or some brewed up magic potion.
When "you" is what you're selling,
You can't beat self promotion.

Don Taylor conceived and co-authored the best seller *Up Against the Wal-Marts* and wrote *Solid Gold Success Strategies for Your Business.* His internationally syndicated business column "Minding Your Own Business" reaches more than one and a half million business readers each week. As a business survival and fast-growth specialist, he speaks regularly to national trade associations, corporate groups, and business organizations. Don can be contacted at 806-236-6513 or on his website at www.dtaylor.com.

Barefoot Marketing

Dana Burke

I have a sign that says, "Life is too short to wear tight shoes." Not as catchy but equally true is, "Business is too important for marketing to be painful." Promoting your business or cause should be as natural and comfortable as kicking off a pair of high heels or wingtips at the end of a long day. That's why I call it "Barefoot Marketing."

In a way, I'm lucky because my parents never taught me that it is bad manners to talk about myself. Instead they taught me to be proud of my talents and accomplishments, and that it is selfish not to share them with others.

So that's where my marketing ideas are based—in the belief that I have something wonderful to offer a potential client, which they won't know if I don't tell them. Shameless? Maybe. But it works, and it's great fun!

> Dana Burke is the founder of Mind Your Business, providing desktop publishing services and marketing communications for micro businesses and small non-profits. She also publishes *Barefoot Marketing*, a free newsletter on marketing your company. Dana has been featured in many publications including *USA Today*, *Success* Magazine, *Business Start-Ups* Magazine and a variety of websites. Dana can be reached at 414-536-7274 or by email at DBurke@execpc.com.

Never Show Them You're Shameless

Rick Segel

The first thing to remember about being a shameless self promoter is not to let anyone know that you are. People hate pushy, loud, obnoxious people who only talk about themselves. However, the key is to have patience. Wait for the right time to say something about yourself. Be humble when people talk about you, but proud of what you have accomplished. Don't say, "I can do that." Instead say, "Let me see if I can help," then blow them away with what you can do. You won't have to talk about yourself, but you will make your listeners into disciples.

Disciples are good. They will do the promoting for you. The way you create disciples is by helping them more than expected, doing a better job than expected, or just becoming their biggest supporter. Your effort will all come back to you. As a baker once told me, "Give it out in slices and it all comes back in loaves." It works!

> Rick Segel, Certified Speaking Professional (CSP), an active retailer for 25 years, is the director of retail training for the Retail Association of Massachusetts. Rick is an internationally recognized speaker who has delivered over 1,400 presentations in 43 states and on three continents. He is the author of *Romancing the Customer, Laugh & Grow Rich, How to Drive Traffic to Your Business*, and *Starting and Running a Retail Business for Dummies*. Rick can be reached at 781-272-9995 or on his website at www.RickSegel.com.

Don't take "NO" for an answer, you either have the wrong audience, or they need more information.

—Debbie Allen

Chapter Two

You Cannot Not Market

Never underestimate the power of your words.
A few select words could motivate others to
"do it now" for many years to follow.
(Note: "Do it now" is a lesson I learned
from Dad and the license plate on my car.)

—Debbie Allen

Shameless Self Promotion Step 2: Keep a Positive Attitude and Contagious Enthusiasm

Debbie Allen

No matter how long you have been in business or how successful your business is, if you stop marketing, you will very quickly see the effects in lost profits and sales. You will lose ground to your competition. In the competitive market today, you simply cannot afford to not market.

I've seen the effects of not marketing first hand. There were times when personal problems affected my mood and, therefore, my self promotion and, eventually, my success. Not only did I have to work harder to build my business back up, I had to work hard to change the mood that had affected my entire business.

Your mood effects your beliefs, which in turn reflects onto your staff and then onto your customers. If you are in a negative mood, it will sweep through your business like a wild fire. Staying positive and enthusiastic is essential to the shameless self promoter. A positive attitude along with contagious enthusiasm will support your groundwork to effectively self promote—even if you think of yourself as a marketing zero. You'll make a good start toward becoming a marketing hero if you have a positive state of mind and contagious enthusiasm.

Self Promote or Disappear!

Larry James

There are several signs in my office that read, "Do something everyday to promote your books and yourself!" Why? It is it so easy to get wrapped up in all the stuff it takes to make my business work that I sometimes forget to promote, promote, promote. So I give myself reminders.

Why self promote? To make sure everyone remembers you. Early in my career I discovered that if I was going to make it, I was the one who was in the best position to do the promotion. I believe in the value of my work in the relationship arena, know my topic better than anyone, and as a result I made a decision to become a do-whatever-it-takes kind of guy—a shameless self promoter. I even talk in elevators.

The first rule of promotion is to talk about your work to anyone and everyone all the time. I do this by being curious and asking questions about what others do. Eventually the conversation shifts to what I do. You call attention to yourself by paying attention to others.

If you don't feel comfortable in promoting your work, get over it! Shy people seldom make it to the top. Be assertive. Speak up. Make sure everyone knows what you do.

Consistency is the key. I've tried just about everything. Some things work. Some don't. However if you think something won't work before you have tried it, you are certain to be right. I would rather be happy and promoting than right…so I will try anything that doesn't compromise my integrity and has worked for someone else. It's exciting to try new ways to promote yourself. It helps make life an adventure.

Once my books were in the book stores I began a relentless campaign to market them. The marketing idea that has reaped the greatest benefit for me has been to appear as a guest on more than 450 radio talk shows. I will talk about my books and the benefits to the radio listeners to any radio host who will have me; large or small markets; for five minutes to a record 2 ½ hour guest shot on a nationally syndicated radio show. I always send the host a signed copy of one of my books and an extra copy as a give-away.

I get an extra plug that way. Many of my radio appearances come from my network of authors/speakers who refer me to radio hosts.

Create a good story with a hook that is informative and entertaining then get yourself booked on lots of talk shows. You have a better chance of getting the interview if you can create a link with what you do to a relevant topic or current event. Always remember—to promote your stuff, you must also provide entertaining content for the radio audience. Talk show hosts will seldom invite you back if you do not first have their audience in mind.

Accept speaking engagements to share helpful information and to promote your business. Afraid to speak in front of groups? Get over it! When you do the thing you fear the most, the death of fear is certain. Make your talk entertaining and informative. Take a speech class or join Toastmasters to fine-tune your speaking skills.

Network for ideas. It has been my experience that successful people are more willing to share their promotional secrets than unsuccessful people. You must ask for what you want. For example, I asked a member of an association I belong to if she would refer me to the producer of ABC TV's The View. She had just completed a guest appearance. She did and I made the cut, an interview with Barbara Walters. Book sales skyrocketed!

Every piece of mail that leaves my office, including the bills that I pay, has my business card and three four-color book marks in it—one for each book. If they can stuff my bill with promotional stuff, so can I. I have received book orders from the people who receive my bill payments. From time to time, I receive offers for subscriptions and various other things. Regardless of whether I am interested in the product or service, if a self-addressed stamped envelope is enclosed, I stuff it with my bookmarks and mail it on my next trip to the post office.

The most exciting part of being a shameless self promoter is sharing my ideas with others. Never be afraid of competition. To me, it doesn't exist. There is plenty of business to go around.

One of my mentors, Sheldon Detrick, once told me that if you ever want to get anywhere in life, you must consistently "put something back!" By that he meant that you must share what you know to help others; become involved in groups and organizations that give you the opportunity to share. I believed him and it has worked for me.

Shel also taught me that you cannot help others, you can only help them help themselves. You can only share what you know with others and they must do something with the information. Use it or lose it.

I love self promotion. I love the excitement of discovering a new idea that introduces more customers to my business. I enjoy brainstorming with others about ideas that have worked for them. Most great promotional ideas can be adapted to your business with a little creativity.

Never pass up an opportunity to promote yourself and your business. If you stop promoting, your business will die a slow death. Never stop.

> Larry James is a professional speaker and author of three relationship books, *Love Notes for Lovers: Words That Make Music for Two Hearts Dancing, How to Really Love the One You're With: Affirmative Guidelines for a Healthy Love Relationship,* and *Red Hot Love Notes for Lovers.* You can contact Larry at 800-725-9223 or view his books and dynamic website at www.CelebrateLove.com.

Not Marketing Can Be Disastrous

Jeff Rubin

The first week of 1992 was a gentle one in the San Francisco Bay Area, unlike the torment of the year before. That January a cold wave (well, cold for Northern Californians!) swept through the area, destroying plants, increasing sales at Eddie Bauer and L.L. Bean, and bringing snow (gasp!) to downtown San Francisco for about a minute and a half.

While the radio bemoaned bumper-to-bumper traffic on clogged freeways, I leisurely took my daily 40-foot commute to my home office, complete with a computer, radio, TV, coffee warmer, and a dog at my feet. Business boomed and I was comfortable, tucked away in my second-floor sanctuary. I belonged to no networking groups, chambers of commerce, or other business or professional organizations. I didn't advertise, didn't promote myself, and did virtually no marketing of any kind. Why bother—I had all the customers I could handle.

"Then one day, for some mysterious reason, we all simultaneously stopped believing our own hype, and the company just went POOF!"

How could I know that my idyllic, isolated working world was setting me up for business failure? January 1992 turned harsh in a big hurry. On successive days that first week I lost two of my three biggest customers. The recession hit California like a sledgehammer, and for the first time in my entrepreneurial career, I felt fear. Would I survive, or would I have to get a real job?

The fact is that 90 percent of businesses fail in the first five years. I wonder what percentage of those simply give up, just throw up their hands and say, "This isn't worth it."

And so I learned my first invaluable business lesson the hard way: No matter how successful you are, no matter how many customers you have, no matter how much the bank account is bulging, you always have to promote yourself. Constantly. Consistently. Continuously. You must be unrelenting in reminding potential customers that you exist. I learned another invaluable lesson with this experience: There's no shame in self promotion if you're promoting something of value.

In the ensuing years I've tried a little bit of everything in my quest for the right promotional mix for my business. Some strategies have worked, some haven't. Below are seven techniques I used to rebuild my business in the nineties. They illustrate the most profound lesson I've learned about self promotion: Who you are means more than what you're promoting.

Seven Guaranteed-to-Work Marketing Strategies

1. Be reliable. This is one of the most important competitive advantages you have.

2. Say "thank you" three times—once over the phone, once in writing, and once in person.

3. Maintain high standards of integrity and excellence. Even people who don't hire you will recommend you.

4. Be a problem solver. This is more important than having a good product or service.

5. Sell value and you'll make more money. Don't charge your customers for every breath you take on their behalf.

6. Don't be cheap. Prospects will respond more readily if you present a polished image.

7. Take a long-term view of your promotional activities. Patience will produce consistent results and steady growth.

One final thought: Spend less time pursuing dollars and more time pursuing relationships. Business success is about relationships, and relationships take time.

> Jeff Rubin, a former newspaper reporter and editor, owns Put It In Writing, a full-service newsletter writing and design firm. He's spent the last 20 years helping companies effectively communicate with their clients and employees, writing and designing more than 1,200 newsletters. Jeff speaks on writing, marketing, and business networking. He can be reached at 877-588-1212 or on his website at www.put-it-in-writing.com.

Using Cold Calls to Make Contacts

Peter Urs Bender and George Torok

Brrrr. Why do they call them "cold" calls? Because the thought of making them sends chills through even the bravest of souls. You might be able to talk on the phone for hours with a friend. But imagine calling someone who doesn't know you from Adam or Eve. You have to explain who you are and why the heck you are calling. You are so afraid you might sound like one of those people who call you at home in the evenings asking to clean your ducts or pave your driveway. The person at the other end of the line might hang up at any second, so you blurt it out and pray. You feel at their mercy.

And what if you are prevented from reaching your cold contact by the dreaded gatekeeper? No problem. Believe in yourself, read the tips below, then start dialing.

> *Fear defeats more people than*
> *any other one thing in the world.*
>
> —Ralph Waldo Emerson

Five Tips to Defrosting Cold Colds

1. **Get Ready to Call.**

   Before you start, have a list of names and numbers ready. No skipping names once you start. Spend time preparing your list before you start calling. You may grow less willing to continue after you get turned down a few times.

   Have everything you need ready before you start: script notes, pricing, calendar, pen, and pad. And visit the bathroom beforehand; you want no distractions.

Get yourself "in the mood." Drink water, rehearse your script, think positively. Stretch, then sit or stand tall and confident. Remind yourself how much that last customer loved your service.

Be clear on why you are calling. Your purpose might be to book a meeting, to discover the contact's short- or long-term needs, to get additional contact names, to introduce yourself, to discover what suppliers they use now, or some combination of these goals.

2. **Schedule a Time Every Day.**

    Don't do anything else during that time period. When one call is finished, dial the next. At the end of the scheduled time period, stop. Better to stop fresh than beat. That way you'll think. "Wow, that wasn't so bad. Can't wait for next time." Set goals and measure what you do. How many is enough will depend on your market and success rate.

3. **Voice Mail Can Be Great.**

    Voice mail will allow you to leave your rehearsed, 30-second message without interruption. In fact, if you call when you know the person you are trying to reach is not available, it may even help you to de-ice the first couple of calls. Leave your phone number twice, once at the start and once at the end of your message.

4. **Get Past the Gatekeeper.**

    Gatekeepers feel protective of their charge. They want to feel valued and important. If you make them feel that way you will get cooperation instead of ice.

5. **A Real Live Person.**

    So now you've finally made your contact with a living, breathing human being. Talk to them, listen attentively, and make notes. Do they sound interested, ambivalent, not interested? After each call, make a quick mental check. Is there anything you should have done differently?

Cold calling is an activity that many people hate, but it works. Don't worry if you don't feel good; you may even feel sick just thinking about it. This is one thing that is worth doing imperfectly and improving. Just start, and keep at it.

> Peter Urs Bender and George Torok, both from Canada, are professional speakers and the authors of *Secrets of P-O-W-E-R Marketing, Promote Brand You.* Over 100,000 copies of the book are in print and used in over forty colleges and universities plus many of the top 500 companies. To learn more about the book and its authors view www.PowerMarketing.ca.

I did it the same way I learned to speak—
by doggedly making a fool of myself
until I got used to it.

—George Bernard Shaw
(on how he became such a compelling speaker)

Fun Ways to Turn Hidden Moments into Marketing Miracles

Debbie Bermont

Keeping on track with your marketing efforts on a year 'round basis can sometimes be a challenge. Do you fall into the dangerous trap of ditching your marketing efforts when your business starts getting busy? Or, even worse, do you practice shotgun-marketing programs implemented only when there is a dip in your sales? These are marketing mistakes that ultimately cost you time and money.

After almost two decades of working with Fortune 500 companies and small businesses across the country, I have found that businesses face the same set of challenges which prevent them from achieving consistent, profitable results from their marketing efforts. It pretty much boils down to lack in one or all of these areas: focus, communication, expertise, time, money, consistency, and commitment. The key to marketing success is year 'round commitment and consistency in keeping in constant communication with your customers (even when they aren't buying from you).

Keeping on track with your marketing on a year 'round basis is really pretty simple. All you need are the right tools and a set of strategies that are easy to implement. The most important tool you need is a personal organizer to house your database. It doesn't matter what you use to house the information, as long as you have a database that is up-to-date with all the names, addresses, and contact information that is accessible to you at all times.

Now you need to find a few moments *every* day to contact people on your database. Now that's a challenge. For the average business owner, marketing falls pretty far down on the totem poll of things to do when you're busy…right below employee management, operations, accounting, production, customer service, etc. But take the time to squeeze a few hidden minutes out of your busy day and you will really start to see your efforts pay off.

Three Fun Ideas that Will Put a Smile on Your Prospect's Face

Fun Idea 1

Airline regulations require you to be at the airport an hour before your flight. Instead of reading a magazine, go to the newspaper stand and buy postcards. Whether it's a postcard from the city you live in or the destination you are traveling to, a picture postcard always gets immediate attention. In an hour you could probably write at least 20 postcards to prospects and customers and mail them in the airport mailbox before you get on the plane. Keep your message light and humorous...the warm fuzzy approach is always memorable.

Fun Idea 2

While you're waiting in your customer's office, ask the receptionist if you can borrow a phone line. Fire up your laptop computer and send five customers an animated greeting card. WWW.Bluemountain.com is the most popular website that has animated greeting cards for every occasion. You can customize a quick message on the greeting card and send it off.

Fun Idea 3

Share your coffee break with your customers. Next time you go to your favorite coffee house, buy small sample packets of coffee. Send them to your customers with a simple note that says "Would love to get together for a cup of coffee with you soon. In the meantime, enjoy the enclosed cup of coffee and have a great day." Chances are your customer will call *you* when they receive this unexpected package to set up a meeting.

Every contact you make is another connection that strengthens profitable customer relationships.

Debbie Bermont, president of Source Communications, a marketing consulting firm, has helped businesses nationwide generate immediate results with her simple marketing approach. For more information about consulting services, speaking programs by Debbie Bermont, business resource tools, and a *free* copy of her e-book, *How To Market Your Business Without Spending A Dime!* contact Debbie at 619-291-6951 or view her website at www.simpleprinciples.com.

Chapter Three

Gutsy Marketing for the Shameless

The most absurd and reckless aspirations have sometimes led to extraordinary success.

—Vauvenargues (great leader of the 1700s)

Shameless Self Promotion Step 3: Develop Gutsy Goals that Make You Stretch

Debbie Allen

Most successful entrepreneurs are always looking for new opportunities. They not only seek them out with keen awareness; they act upon them. They thrive on taking chances they strongly believe in. Your next opportunity may seem a little crazy, a little far-fetched—even scary. But don't let that hold you back! If your goals aren't at least a little scary they are probably not stretching you enough.

When writing this book, a few people told me that they don't market and that they do not consider themselves self promoters, much less shameless. This amazed me. These are successful business people, and they don't market? How could that be? Those lucky few—and I do mean few—are extremely talented people. They may not realize it, but when they showcase their talents, they are self promoting. Those of us who are not as gifted may just need to work a lot harder at it. We need to shamelessly let the world know who we are and why they need to do business with us.

Are you ready to develop some gutsy goals? Are you ready to take a chance on your own success?

Sometimes that's just what it takes to make it happen. If you don't step up and take a chance now and then you will never see your highest level of success. The world is full of people who are too scared to take chances. Those people keep saying "what if..." Maybe you've even caught yourself saying, "What if it doesn't work out?" "What if I fail?" "What if...?" "What if...?"

If you want to be a shameless self promoter you must change "what if" to "what if I don't?" What if I don't make that intimidating marketing call? What if I don't take a risk on a gutsy idea from time to time? What if I don't get past my fear and do something new and a little scary to promote myself?

You've all heard the saying, "If you don't ask, you don't get." I'll add to that: "If you don't take a chance, you will never reap the rewards!" The rewards include growing your business to another level of success and gaining a much stronger belief in yourself and your abilities.

Come to the Edge: Self Promoter from Within

Melanie Roetken

"If you are not living on the edge, you're taking up too much space." I recently heard that gem of wisdom and I wish I knew to whom I should give proper credit. It must have been a shameless self promoter, because when it comes to advancing one's image in the business world, living on the edge and having the guts to seize opportunities when you see them is what it's really all about. Why? Because if we want to grow our businesses in creative new ways, we must step out of our comfort zone and take risks. It starts from within and is, quite simply, an attitude!

As a business owner, that indefinable risk-taking quality has served me well over the years and, in my mind, is the very core of effective self promotion. Upon reflection, I've found that taking the time to assess your individual strengths on a regular basis and then stretch yourself to go a little further is of utmost importance.

Every person has qualities that set them apart, so capitalize on your own natural gifts and let that shine through in all your promotions. The self confidence you project will take you to even bigger dreams and will ultimately act like a magnet that attracts your potential audience. My belief is that a self confident—not ego driven—attitude communicates your own personal passion and style and becomes the very foundation for overcoming obstacles. You will be unstoppable, for it is true that success feeds on success. An attitude of self confidence coupled with a passion for your product or service is the irresistible combination.

I have never been described as an "in your face" self promoter. Yet my businesses have always prospered because I found unique and sincere ways to forge a memorable connection with my target audience. One promotion idea that took on a life of its own was sending an unusual custom Christmas card each year to my database of customers and vendors. I quickly found that a side benefit to creating an eye-catching card was that many companies display the Christmas cards they receive around the holidays so others can enjoy. If you think of all promotions as a form of advertising, each year the number of positive impressions you can make with a creative Christmas card will multiply tenfold.

The most memorable card was the year that I asked a famous New York caricature artist to turn my idea into reality. During a business trip to the Big Apple, quite by accident I met Vic Cantone, former political cartoonist for the New York Times who was moonlighting at an elegant revolving restaurant overlooking Broadway in Manhattan. After having my own caricature done just for fun, the idea flashed across my mind. Why not use his talent to help create a Christmas card that promoted my two travel-related companies. To my amazement he agreed and the rest is history. In spite of geographic challenges and a short lead time, the finished project generated rave reviews.

Before you set forth your own marketing/publicity plan to sell yourself to the world, stop and take a personal inventory of what makes you and your company truly unique. With a solid foundation of healthy self confidence and a can-do attitude, you will be forearmed and ready when the inherent risks of business ownership surface. Better yet, when forced to the edge, you will fly.

Melanie Roetken is an entrepreneur, freelance writer, business consultant, marketing and public relations specialist, realtor, and world traveler. She founded Phoenix and Tucson Flight Guides and Condo Vacations of Arizona. Now in real estate, she is building her third business—helping individuals find their vacation dream home both on-site and on-line. Contact Melanie by email at mroetken@amug.org or visit her website at www.isellvacationhomes.com.

> *Come to the edge, she said.*
> *I said, I can't, I might fall.*
> *Come to the edge, she said.*
> *I said, I can't, I am afraid.*
> *Come to the edge, she said*
> *I came, she pushed me. And I flew.*
>
> —Author unknown

Hustle if You Want to Be Great

Willie Jolley

When I was starting my speaking business I went to a conference in Nashville to learn more about the speaking business. While there I heard about another conference going on across town, the National Association of College Activities (NACA) Conference. I knew a friend who regularly spoke at that conference and called his mother to see if he was speaking that year as well. She told me he was and gave me a number to contact him.

I called him and told him I was in town and would love to come over and learn about this college market firsthand. He told me to come over but said that the main activities would not start for another day, but I was welcome to share his room overnight. I jumped on the opportunity because I had only $75 to change my plane reservation and about $25 for a couple of cheap meals.

When we got together he took me around the convention and explained how the process worked. He explained that college student activities directors came to this conference to look for new speaking talent and would go from showcase to showcase to hear new talent. I asked, "How do you get to showcase? Can I?" He laughed and said those decisions were made months in advance and all the showcases had long been filled, plus he said that I would need to register and pay a fee just to get into the showcase rooms. This immediately put me out of the running! He told me that he recommended I just play it cool and he would introduce me to a few of the "right" people and maybe I could showcase at the next year's convention.

But I couldn't wait until next year. I needed to get this going right now! The next morning I woke up early and got my little flyers and stood outside the showcase doors. I gave everybody who was going in a flyer and said, "Ever need a speaker, please call me!" A short while later my friend came up and pulled me to the side and said, "You can't do that. You'll never get booked like that, plus you are embarrassing yourself as well as me." He walked in the room and once he was gone...I started again. "If you ever need a speaker..."

A while later my friend was back after seeing people still come in with my flyers. This time he was really mad and told me I was cutting my own throat and I had better stop or I would be seen as a jerk and would totally embarrass myself as well as him. But again as soon as he was gone...I started again, until I ran out of flyers. Later that day I was walking through the halls and a gentleman came up to me and asked if I was the one who had the nerve to give out flyers without even registering. I was kind of afraid but I gave him a sheepish "Yes." He said, "I've been looking for you since this morning. I am the president of the College Speaking Bureau and I like your style. Here's my card, please send me your stuff." A few weeks later he was booking me to colleges all over the country. By the way, the college agent did not sign my friend, who was too cool to hustle!

> *Good things go to those who wait,*
> *but you must hustle if you want to be great.*
> *Hustle and don't be ashamed.*
> *Be proud about it!*
>
> Willie Jolley

Willie Jolley is an award-winning speaker, singer, and author. He was named one of the Outstanding Five Speakers in the World by Toastmasters International. He is the author of two best-selling books, *It Only Takes a Minute to Change Your Life* and *A Setback Is a Setup for a Comeback*. He is also the host of the syndicated radio and television show, *The Magnificent Motivational Minute!* Willie can be reached at 800-487-8899. For a free minute of motivation, call 888-266-8488 or view Willie's website at www.WillieJolley.com.

Happy Birthday to Me

Raleigh Pinskey

There I was, an addition to the moving masses, elevated egos, and the snobby social strata in my newly adopted home of New York City. Shy is not an adjective you would use to describe me. Yet there I was having a difficult time breaking through the political layers of dues paying and territorial markings of the members of the clubs and organizations in which I wanted sandbox privileges.

I had what I thought were acceptable credentials—a good paying job with a title, a quick mind, great networking skills, and a right-on-NY-banter patter. I was in my late twenties with looks that attracted attention and an approved address on the upper East Side. But no matter how much volunteer time I put in, I couldn't get past the first level of dues paying wherever I went. Here I was, the CEO of my own PR and marketing company representing some of the "hottest" celebrities in the entertainment industry, and my own publicity was going nowhere.

To add insult to injury, I now spent my birthdays alone. And as one's birthday always does, there it was again, looming directly in my face. I thought about taking myself to Chucky Cheese, but nixed the idea even before it bloomed. It was my thirtieth, and I was compelled not to spend it with my usual date, the waiters at my favorite Chinese restaurant around the corner.

There I was, a double Gemini (Gemini, the twins, is May 15 to June 15, and I had a sun sign and a rising sign in Gemini). That meant that four of me were all dressed up with no place to go on my birthday.

My morose self-pity brought me to the thought of having a pity party. I'd invite the girls and we'd celebrate our low self-esteem and unfulfilled, lonely lives.

The concept of throwing a birthday party for myself was a no-no in the social etiquette lineage of my family. Throw a party for yourself? And let everyone know you had no one to throw it for you? This was a bad thing.

No sooner had I had the thought than I registered it loud and clear. Let lineage be buried, I am going to throw myself a birthday party. And if I'm alone, there must be other Geminis with no place to go or no one to celebrate with.

I called all my Gemini girlfriends and invited them to a party at my house. For my present, I asked them each to bring another Gemini girlfriend so we could increase our networking potential. The first Gemini party embraced twenty wonderful women. The second year I stopped counting after forty.

By now the word was out on me. I began getting calls to join certain organizations that had been closed to me, as well as calls to join committees that had passed over me. Power breakfast and lunch invitations came in from both female and male movers and shakers. My client roster increased and my name quotient grew in my social and professional community. When people introduced me they included, "You know Raleigh, she has that well-known PR company that represents Blondie, Sting, and Paul McCartney, and she's also the woman who throws that fantastic Gemini Party, that wonderful networking opportunity where very interesting women can be found."

By the third year I was getting requests from women I didn't know who wanted to be invited. And as long as they were Geminis they were welcome. It was BYO (bring your own food and drinks) and the gourmet take-out that showed up on my table made it truly a feast from NY's finest.

The fourth year proved the proverb that necessity is the mother of invention. Women called and said, "I have a Gemini rising," or "I have a Gemini moon," or "I have a planet in Gemini," and asked if they could come to the party. And so the party was blessed with more wonderful women.

By the fifth year I had moved to a larger apartment and it was a good thing because I was getting requests from people from out of town who would schedule business if they could come. And was it glorious. The apartment was filled with all shapes, sizes, and colors of great women who had great stories to tell and wonderful toasts to give.

The party lasted two more years and then I moved to Los Angeles. Of course I did the same thing there to break into the social arena.

The idea came full circle with two occurrences. I got a call that first year from a woman I didn't know who had just moved from NY to LA. Before she left NY her friend, whom I also didn't know, told her to look me up as soon as she got there to see if she could get an invite to my Gemini Party. If it was anything like the one in NY, she said, she was bound to get an introduction into a crowd of great LA people.

The second heartwarming thing occurred when I got a wedding invitation from a couple who had met at my Gemini Party.

To this day people come up and tell me that they either were at my party, knew of people who were, or heard about it and wished they had known about it sooner. I tell them to come to LA.

Aside from the networking, the friends, and the name recognition, I learned some very valuable lessons from this experience. One, don't listen if someone tells you that it is not proper to throw yourself a birthday party, and two, share that special day with others. It will make them happy and you happy too. And we all know how warm and contagious happiness is. That one day of honoring each other turned into a 365-day continuous joy.

Happy Birthday everyone, and many happy returns.

> Raleigh Pinskey is CEO of the Raleigh Group, a Viz-Ability PR & Marketing Company, a PR marketing consultant and a professional speaker. Raleigh is the best-selling author of *101 Ways to Promote Yourself* and six books on how to use the media to your business advantage. Contact Raleigh at 800-249-7322 or view her website at www.PromoteYourself.com.

The RV Adventure Book Tour

Greg Godek

See what everyone else is doing and then do something different with an innovative and creative mindset. That's what I base all of my marketing efforts upon today.

When I began publishing romantic-oriented relationship books, I knew that I wanted to own the positioning of "romantic love." I want people to think of Greg Godek or *1001 Ways to Be Romantic* when they think about love and romance. When you think of someone who writes about sex, for example, you instantly think of Dr. Ruth. It has been her positioning in the marketplace; she "*owns*" sex." Dr. Ruth has branded her name; in fact, her name is more important than the titles to her books. I have a number of her books, and I couldn't tell you the title for any of them. But her name is recognized around the world. Other authors who are at this level of self-branding include Steven King for horror and Danielle Steel for fictional romance. They have branded themselves on the specific topics.

It's much harder to brand your name than your product. When I started out I was an unknown, so I needed to brand my book's concept. To brand my book I knew that whatever I did, I must be creative, outrageous, and, most of all, relentless.

Now don't get me wrong, if you don't do your core marketing first, your outrageous marketing won't work. You have four choices when it comes to marketing.

1. Do it yourself (and shamelessly)

2. Hire it out (an expensive but easy option)

3. Flail around (or)

4. Just fail!

If you think you are just too logical a person to think of anything creative, then at least hire someone to get the job done for you. Find a marketing person, PR person, or a college intern, but find somebody. Don't just sit there—because somebody else will pass you by.

When my book first came out, I did my core marketing and enjoyed a great deal of media coverage for my book. I had been on *Oprah, Donahue, Jenny Jones* and *Montel*. Now, I wanted my book to *keep* selling well, so I had to lift my efforts to another level. That's how I came up with my RV adventure book tour.

A standard book tour in the publishing business consists of ten to 20 cities. Many publishers think of the tour as simply a book signing with some media exposure. They usually don't make much money because of this mindset. Contrary to that, I don't like being standard. I like doing things better, bigger, and more creatively. Since the media is so important in the promotion of any business, I knew that if I were going to have a shot at the media, I had to make it my best shot. I would rather reach 100,000 people at a time than the ten to 20 people that come into a book signing. That was my inspiration to begin thinking outside of the box—way outside of the box.

Back in 1995 I saw an article in the newspaper that showed an entire city bus shrink-wrapped in an advertisement. I thought, "Wow! This is something new and innovative. What does this ad-wrapped bus have to do with my publishing business? I don't know yet, but it's a cool idea." I cut out the article and put it in my "crazy marketing ideas" file for future reference.

Meanwhile, I was getting tired of going to a different city every day for weeks for my Valentine's Day media tour. I had done this same thing for years, and I spent around $20,000 in just three weeks flying all over the place. I stopped for a while to think about what else I could do. What else could I spend my time, money, and creativity on?

First, I looked at my entire marketing budget as one lump sum. I started considering all my options. I asked myself, "What can I do in the future to make my marketing efforts more effective?" One day during a brainstorming session, the phrase "50 states in 50 weeks" hit me. Wow! What a great concept! Wouldn't it be cool to visit all 50 states in 50 weeks? I could fly — but it would cost too much money and I wouldn't have much time to do interviews and drop into bookstores in different cities. How else could I do it effectively? Ah ha! If I'm going to do all 50 states I'm going to need a motor home.

I had never been in an RV in my life, and the concept of living in one was a completely foreign to me. So at first I thought, "How can I buy a motor home and travel all over the country? What am I going to do, just pick up and be gone for a couple of years? My wife works! We own a home! This won't work! It's a crazy idea; it needs to be filed away. This does not even go in my Crazy Marketing Ideas file because it's simply *ridiculous!*"

Just as I was about to file the idea forever, the shrink-wrap idea came back to me. My thoughts went from the ridiculously impossible to "Wow, would that look great on a motor home! I could design the entire thing featuring the cover of my book. Wouldn't that be outrageous!"

It's a funny thing, but no matter how insane an idea may appear at the moment, a great idea simply won't go away. So—to make a long story short—I bought the 36-foot RV. My wife left her job to travel along with me; we rented out our house and hit the road for two years. We traveled to nearly all 50 states by crossing the country four times. This included a nightmare drive through downtown New York City in a snowstorm to appear on Good Morning America (but that is a story in itself).

Not only was this crazy and gutsy, it was also financially risky. I purchased a $100,000 RV and hired a professional designer for another $14,000 without being able to realistically calculate the financial return on my investment. I had no idea at the time that it would turn out to be the biggest book tour in the history of the world. This is just an example of how a small- to medium-size business can compete with the big guys. The big guys could never be this creative or take this much risk and spend this much time and money on something that they could not measure the results of beforehand.

To be an effective self promoter you must know your most valuable resources. The three resources at your disposal are time, money, and creativity. Most people take the easy way out and just spend the money. Others that don't have the money sometimes put out negative energy and excuses by stating that they can't afford to make a big difference in promoting their business. Yet, anyone can afford to put in energy, time, and creativity. Most people are just not doing enough creative things to market their business. To be more creative, start to think about crazy ideas that can be adjusted to fit your business. Create your own Crazy Marketing Ideas file. Trust me, you will never run out of ideas. If you don't feel comfortable stepping out of your comfort zone to outrageous, shameless self marketing, get over it!

> Greg Godek is the author of the best-selling *1001 Ways to Be Romantic* (1.7 million copies sold). Greg is a consultant who works with authors who want to be bestsellers. He also presents romance seminars in his spare time. Contact Greg at 858-456-7177 or find out more about his book and/or seminars at www.Godek.com

Shameless Marketing Gets into the Act

Silvana Clark

I gained my marketing experience by trying to make my dog "famous." I was obsessed with getting "Sherman the Wonder Dog" on television commercials. With no marketing experience at all, I got him spots on commercials for Honda, Chrysler, Reebok, and many others. I then began doing workshops on innovative marketing ideas because the concepts I used to market Sherman are easily adapted to small businesses.

Knowing that most people have a soft spot for dogs, I marketed myself by including Sherman's 8" x 10" glossy in my marketing portfolio. Then, when talking with a client, I'd mention that I could bring Sherman along to my presentation. They were thrilled! (I often ended up with second billing.) I'd go to a conference, give a presentation, and then let the audience shake Sherman's paw. It was comical to see adults in business suits line up to shake paws with a dog. But it got me work!

Sherman is now frolicking in doggie heaven, and I've moved on to my next marketing tool—my daughter. As an 11 year old, Sondra has had two craft books published by major publishers and distributed by Simon and Schuster. But everyone in marketing knows you have to do something different to get the media's attention. It wasn't enough that Sondra had written two books; she is also very articulate in front of groups. I've gotten her appearances on the *Donny and Marie Show*, the *700 Club, Crook and Chase*, and numerous craft-related shows, In addition major magazines and newspapers have written about her. Now, when groups ask me to speak, I mention that for an additional fee, I can bring Sondra along. Groups love having a "celebrity" and enjoy hearing her experiences. (Face it, most of the women just want to know what it was like meeting Donny Osmond. Not!) Naturally we sell our books at the back of the room with great success.

So, first I marketed my dog, and now I'm on to my daughter. My clients and audiences want something different, whether it be a dog or a cute kid. As a shameless promoter, I give them what they want.

Silvana Clark is a professional speaker and award-winning author. She travels around the world presenting seminars on innovative marketing ideas. She's often accompanied by her 11-year-old daughter, Sondra, herself the author of two books and busy on the talk show circuit. Silvana Clark can be reached at 360-734-9506 or view her website at www.SilvanaClark.com.

Don't Miss an Opportunity to Be Shameless

Natalie Buske Thomas

I learned that Governor Jesse Ventura was stopping in our town (a small town of under 4,000 people) on his Tour 2000. I called city hall to ask where the Gov would be.

Just minutes before I found out the location, I grabbed my two-year-old son and put clothes on him, but I forgot his underwear. By the time I realized this, there was no time to go back, so I just kept moving. I didn't have time to shower or do my hair, so I threw my hair back and used that power freeze hair spray stuff to fake it. I wasn't dressed very well, so I grabbed my red wool dress coat, which completely covered me. Voila! Showerless me and my *al fresco* son were ready to meet the governor of Minnesota.

I missed his appearance. He was leaving the local bar, where he had invited the public to meet him. We (husband, two kids, and I) saw the tour bus pulling away. But I remembered something about a factory tour, so we took off for the factory. When I showed up he was on a tour with area businessmen. I said that I was hoping to get the Gov's autograph. Ventura's bodyguards saw my children and agreed to let us stay and wait for him to finish the tour.

At the end of the tour, the governor was surrounded by a mob of press. He was on his way out the door when I reached out and said, "Governor? Could I get your autograph for my kids?" He hesitated for a second, then said, "Sure." The press cleared a path for me, then I walked up to him. I didn't have any paper with me, so I helped myself to a piece that was lying around the factory office. I thought, Ooh, I've sunk so low, now I'm stealing copier paper.

Then I offered him my book. I told him that I signed it to First Lady Ventura, and that the money that Governor Ventura got for us Minnesotans in the form of a tax rebate was used to attend a trade show to promote this book. Suddenly the cameras were snapping and I was drawn into the circle, getting my picture taken with our famous governor.

This went better than my wildest dreams! I was hoping only to get a quote from him to use on my website. I never dreamt that it would become my 15 minutes of fame. Later, a blurb about my visit with the governor was posted to the Gov's official website. I posted my pictures of the visit on my own website. I continue to get attention from that one gutsy encounter.

Shameless, shameless! A soft-spoken and reserved person, I am amazed that I did something so gutsy—it was like I was watching someone else do it!

Natalie Buske Thomas is the author of *The Pizza Loving Detective*, *Serena Wilcox Mysteries* (for adult readers) and *The Magic Camera* mystery/fantasy series for children. For more information about her books and resources for entrepreneurs, contact Natalie at Natalie@independentmysteries.com or view her website at www.IndependentMysteries.com.

Redirecting Shameless Marketing Energies

Jim Cathcart

Years ago I was a $500 a month government clerk for the Little Rock Housing Authority. I had no college degree, no money in the bank, and a wife and a new baby at home. Feeling like there was no way out of this financial mess, I realized that I must start to shamelessly promote myself.

I had previously worked in the banking business and had always been impressed with bankers. It was my dream to be a banker and have a nice respectable office. So I took my shameless self down to the trust office to speak to an officer. "I want to become a trust officer," I stated. The banker came back with a difficult question. "What are your credentials?" Well, I had to admit that I had none, but that I truly wanted to be a trust officer, and I would appreciate his guidance to accomplish this. He saw through my shamelessness and realized that I was sincere. He gave me a book from the American Institute of Banking and told me to take it home and read it, then give him a call.

Two days later I called him back. He said, "No, wait to call me until after you have read the entire book." I assured him that I had finished reading the huge book from cover to cover. I asked him to quiz me on it. After asking me a couple of questions, he could see that I had done my homework. He then set up another meeting with me and, over the next few weeks, basically gave me a banking course with his help and support. That led me to getting an interview with the bank.

At the same time, my luck started to turn around at my existing job. I was offered a promotion to staff assistant for the board of directors, which I decided to take. My fellow employees elected me president of the Employees Association as a joke, but I took the role seriously. I gathered my new-found shameless marketing energies and redirected them into this new job. I really started asserting myself. Shortly after getting the promotion I went into the boss's office and told him that I knew of several ways that we could improve the organization but that we would need to make some changes. Then I handed him a three-page plan of action. He was so impressed he not only implemented the plan, but he gave me a raise right on the spot. I have been committed to shameless self promotion ever since.

Self promotion requires a different mindset than most people are used to. You need to think of yourself as a brand or a product. That's not always easy to do. In the legal or medical fields a lot of people feel that it is wrong to put yourself out there with a bold marketing message. But times are changing, even within those industries.

As a speaker, the key to my success has been to have people think of me as the product. If you can separate your thinking of "you" from your ego long enough to notice your strengths and weaknesses, you can think of them objectively. Then, and only then, you can do some real useful planning as to how to optimize your opportunities.

> Jim Cathcart is a leader among speakers. Jim is past president of the National Speakers Association, Speaker Hall of Fame member, Cavett Award winner, and author of 12 books, including *The Acorn Principle*. Jim is CEO of Cathcart Institute, Inc. and a psychological researcher/business strategist with 23 years of professional speaking experience. Jim can be reached at 858-456-3813 or view his website at www.Cathcart.com.

Thank Heaven for Little Girls

T. J. Reid

I was in my mid-twenties (too many years ago to mention) when I opened my first ladies clothing store in my hometown in Louisiana. Being a shameless self promoter, even back then, I named the store after me, calling it T.J.'s for Her.

That was my first shameless step toward success. The local town gossips were always talking about the fashionable new store, opened by that young girl who moved to town. The store's name, and my name was on everyone's lips! I began to realize that everywhere I went, I was not just T.J. Reid, but now I was "the store," a representation of what every woman expected when shopping at T.J.'s for Her. I was careful to have myself and my employees always look the part.

As I entered my second year of business, my husband and I were thrilled to discover that I was pregnant. It didn't stop me from working, it just changed the way I did some things. In my monthly newsletters I kept customers updated on my due date. We held a contest to guess if the baby was a girl or a boy and the closest birth date and time. Winners received gift certificates from my store. It made them feel involved in my pregnancy, thus building a loyal following.

People warned me about how much business I would lose because I would not be able to devote as much time to my work. Boy, were they wrong. It only made business better. Customers came in just to check on me and later the baby, whom I kept in a crib in the back near my office. (I was way ahead of my time on bringing my child to work.) While customers were giggling and tickling the newborn, I was filling their shopping bags with the latest new fashions.

After my precious little girl arrived, I used her in my advertisements. I dressed her in a bikini and announced "Swimwear Has Arrived at T.J's!" I placed her inside a pumpkin (way before Anne Geddes thought of it) and announced "Come In and Pick a Pumpkin Discount for our Halloween Sale!"

The best ad I did was for my daughter's first Christmas. I dressed her up in a holiday bonnet and had her face photographed in the center of a large Christmas wreath, The headline read, "Merry Christmas from My Mommy's Store!" This ad won a prize from the Louisiana Press Association and many years later was featured in my book, *What Mother Never Told Ya about Retail*. Oh, yes, the little girl? She's now 27 years old and has a little darling of her own. Another marketing miracle is born!

T.J. Reid was an award-winning fashion retailer for over 20 years. She also served as on-air personality for the QVC Home Shopping Network before launching a career as an author and professional speaker. An accomplished journalist, she has garnered over 20 national press awards for her business articles and books. A popular Southern humorist and fashion guru, she has presented over 1,500 programs throughout the country for women from ages 18-80, "Fashion, Fun, & Feelings: A Lady Looks at Life!" T.J. can be reached at 800-221-8615 or on the web at www.tjreid.com.

If you obey all the rules you miss all the fun.

—Katherine Hepburn

Chapter Four

Shameless Friends and Associates

*You can make more friends in two months
by becoming interested in other people than
you can in two years by trying to
get other people interested in you.*

—Dale Carnegie

Shameless Self Promotion Step 4: Seek Out and Act on Opportunities

Debbie Allen

If you have read this far and still think it is too hard to promote yourself, this chapter is for you. You will learn how to coach others to shamelessly promote you. Your friends, family, customers and business associates already love you, why not ask them to continue supporting you and your business through referrals.

There are three easy steps to creating glowing testimonials. The first is to simply be aware. We all love compliments. Next time you receive one don't just say thank you. Look the complimentor straight in the eye and say, "I appreciate your noticing, that's so nice. A great testimonial like that could be so helpful to my business. Would you mind writing it down for me on your letterhead? Thank you!"

The second step is to use these testimonials to promote your business and make new prospects into clients. Testimonials are one of the easiest, most effective, and lowest cost promotion tools.

Step three is to reap the benefits with increased exposure and a more profitable business.

Don't fight your competition; join forces. One of my top-selling seminar topics to the retail industry is *How to Compete and Succeed Against the Retail Giants*. What does this tell you? That everyone is concerned about losing ground and their share of the marketplace. It has become a sharky-shark world out there. Everyone is fighting the competition to stay alive. But why fight them, when you can join forces and make them a strategic alliance or associate.

The best thing I did to grow my business to the next level last year was to join forces with one of my toughest competitors, Tom Shay. (See Tom's confession on page 173.) Tom is a professional speaker who specializes in the same niche market that I do. Although I have always been friendly with Tom, I had never thought of actually forming an association with him.

Tom approached me with the idea of sharing our entire leads list, a list we had both worked very hard to develop. At first I was not too keen on the idea. I have always carefully guarded this list from what I used to call "the enemy, " my competition. Sharing my entire leads database was something I had never thought about. Tom, on the other hand, had been doing this with another speaker, Jack Rice, and it had brought them both success. After Jack passed away, Tom especially felt not only the loss of friendship, but also the loss of a dynamic business connection. He longed to build another strong competitive association. He looked for the opportunity and I appeared.

Tom and I more than doubled our database of leads overnight, opened up new market areas, and put our foot in the doors of many new opportunities for our speaking, writing, and consulting business. I can't take every speaking engagement, and neither can Tom, so we are the first to refer one another. This association grew our businesses quickly, increased our credibility, supported our clients, and improved our service.

You never know where and when business will come your way. Seek a referral from your competition for this referral is often perceived as one of the best forms of flattery. For example, while visiting my favorite office supply store, Office Depot, a few weeks ago, I noticed that they were planning to close this particular store (one of 70 bad locations across the nation). I told them how disappointed I was, and that I would miss the friendly and helpful staff. The girl behind the counter said, "We appreciate that, and we will miss you. But when we close I recommend you go to Office Max, not the other office supply store down the street. They are very helpful as well, and I'm sure you will be happy with their service. We don't recommend the other store."

I asked a few more questions and discovered that representatives from Office Max periodically stopped in at Office Depot. The reps checked on what the competition was offering and compared notes. They were always friendly and announced who they were. Over time the staff at the two stores had built a friendly alliance. They would never have known at the time, but they had opened up an incredible opportunity for their future business growth. The referrals from a closing business quickly and dramatically increased their sales. With growing sales they needed more staff. Where do you think they got them? Right! From the competition. The other competitor missed a huge opportunity!

When you help and support others it comes back to you many times over in increased referrals, respect, and more business than you can handle. So stop worrying about your competition. Don't fight 'em; join 'em!

The Magic of Referrals

Marilyn Ross

According to a survey of 900 sales and marketing professionals conducted by the Nierenberg Group, referrals are the most effective technique for attracting new customers. The message to entrepreneurs and sale professionals is that the shortest path to new business comes from reviewing existing contacts and asking them to recommend you to others. It's a fact the leads that convert to sales at the highest percentage are referrals from current customers.

Although testimonials many be as good as money in the bank, referrals are money in the bank. Once you've honed you referral approach, I can almost guarantee your bank balance will blossom. A referral is simply one happy client or customer telling another. It is word-of-mouth praise.

> Marilyn Ross is the award-winning author of the new book, *Shameless Marketing for Brazen Hussies: 307 Awesome Money-Making Strategies for Savvy Entrepreneurs*. Ross dipped her toe into entrepreneurial waters at age nine and has run a multitude of successful companies ever since. A marketing consultant and professional speaker, Marilyn can be reached at 719-395-2459 or by visiting her website at www.brazenhussiesnetwork.com.

Let Your Fans Do the Talking

Robert Davis

If you just can't get the courage to promote yourself, then don't. Do what I do: Get your fans to promote you. Now, I don't mind promoting myself but others can do it so much better. That is, the results I get are so much better when others promote me. Hence, a majority of my promotional effort is focused on identifying, recruiting, and inspiring my fans to tell others wonderful things about me.

Seven Steps to Get Fans to Promote You

Step 1: Identify and make a list of your fans.

Your fans represent the people who have demonstrated that they value your products and services. They are the individuals who give you testimonials and referrals, and rate you high on evaluations and customer satisfaction surveys. Your fans are the ones that think you are, as Tony the Tiger would say, "GRREEAT."

Get in the habit of soliciting feedback from each individual who has had an opportunity to sample your products and/or services. The individuals who are the most enthusiastic and who believe that their investment in your products and/or services was a very good decision, are the individuals you should recruit as your fans.

Also, get in the habit of identifying the source of every positive statement made about you and of every referral you receive. When you hear people say positive things about you and your company, write their name and comments down on your list of fans.

Step 2: Outline your promotional message.

In order for your fans to do the best job in promoting you, they will need your help. Your fans will ask you what you want them to say about you, so be prepared. What do you want your fans to say about you? What do you want your fans to say about your products and/or services? Take a moment to make a list of a few sentences and phrases that you would like your fans to tell others about you. Example: "I highly recommend that you get a copy of Robert's book or shop at Jane's store."

Step 3: Ask your fans for feedback.

If you are clear about what you want your fans to say about you, you'll know the right questions to ask them when you gather feedback from them. Once you receive their response to your questions, assuming it is very favorable response, you can ask them to share their experience with others. Their comments can be presented in a letter of recommendation, a written or verbal testimonial statement, or included in promotional literature.

Step 4: Ask for help.

The simplest way to obtain promotional support is to ask. There are several things your fans can do to help promote you and your business. For example, they can help you run a booth at a trade show, display your literature in their office, or nominate you for an award.

Make it as easy as possible for your fans to promote you. For example, you can provide your fans with sample letters of recommendation loaded with examples of the types of statements you want them to say about you. Avoid making it necessary for your fans to pay for expenses related to promoting you.

Step 5: Promote your fans.

A major key to obtaining promotional support is to provide your fans with promotional support. Seek every opportunity to contribute to the success of your prospective fans. Provide them with information, contacts, ideas, resources, and referrals. Your fans will be more willing to promote you the more you contribute to their success. A word of caution: Only promote fans that you respect and believe in. Whatever you say must be truthful.

Step 6: Praise and reward your fans.

Show your appreciation to anyone you discover saying wonderful things about you and your company.

At a minimum, send a thank you note or card. Your acknowledgment will encourage them to continue to provide specifics when speaking about you in the future.

Step 7: Stay in touch and hang out with your fans.

The more you communicate with your fans the more they will tell others about you. Through staying in touch you will learn about opportunities, changes, and plans that you otherwise would not have known. I further recommend that you communicate with your fans, in a quality way, at least every 30 to 60 days.

One of the smartest things you can do to get your fans to promote you is simply to hangout with them. Go to events where one or more of your fans will be attending. Rather than concentrating your effort on meeting new people, spend time hanging out with your fans. Your fans will introduce you to people they know and will usually say a few wonderful things about you. It is a lot easier to meet new people when a fan is introducing you. The words of your fans will be viewed as more objective and truthful than any of the words you could have shared with them about you and your business.

Let your fans know in advance that you are planning to visit with them. Providing them with an advance notice will give them an opportunity to tell others about your upcoming visit.

Word-of-mouth promotion is one of the most powerful and effective methods that you can use to promote yourself. If you just can't get up the nerve to promote yourself, then hang out with the individuals who love you and let them shamelessly tell the world about what you have to offer and how wonderful you are.

> Robert Davis is a professional speaker, trainer, and coach. He is the author of *Implement Now, Perfect Later*, and co-author of *Business by Referral*. He is a contributing author to *Masters of Networking* and *Confessions of Shameless Self Promoters*. Robert is also founder of the Recovering Perfectionist Club. Contact Robert at 909-681-0686 or view his website at www.RobertDavisAssoc.com.

Building Success on Referrals and Testimonials

Sally Hayes

In 1977 I saw acrylic nails being applied in California. I thought, "What a concept, ten perfect nails." At that time the price was $40 a set. I enrolled in beauty school, got my license, and set up shop. I built my business by offering nails, free of charge, to the girls that worked in a restaurant near my shop as long as they would spread the word. I built an instant clientele as well as a great referral base.

I expanded my business to a full service salon with an attached boutique carrying higher-end accessories and clothes. I offered all the salon clients a 20 percent discount on any day they had a salon service. Not only was the retail successful, but it kept my salon on the top. In the mid-eighties, when colored leather was popular, I bought leather pants for size samples, took special orders on outfits, and sold over $40,000 in one season. I pre-sold, took a deposit, and used the client's money to fund the special orders. I did the same with custom knit sweaters. The company could not believe the volume of business I was doing. I was their highest ordering customer in the entire nation that year.

In 1988, 11 years after starting with acrylic nails, I pioneered permanent make-up. Once again I got my salon employees to let me tattoo them, and I was off on a new career. The public had *no idea* that they could have natural looking make-up that wouldn't smear, smudge, or rub off! Therefore, I used clients like Debbie Allen (now you know her secret) to be my ambassador by running their photos and testimonials in a local magazine. Soon word got around and I am now teaching my technique as well as providing permanent make-up for many plastic surgeons in the U.S. and internationally.

You can be as successful as you can imagine by opening your mind and setting your fears aside. If you have never failed you can't possibly succeed, so step out of your box.

> Sally Hayes founded Beauty that Never Fades, Inc. to continue her growth and development of the permanent make-up industry. Sally provides services for prominent plastic surgeons around the nation. She has been featured in *Town and Country* and *Allure* magazines. Sally can be reached at 480-951-0539 or view website at www.PermanentMakeup.com.

Anything Is Pez™-able!

Dana Burke

Most small businesses thrive on word-of-mouth marketing. But few business owners remember to thank those who pass along their name. Mind Your Business has a unique "thank you" system for referrals. When someone says that they gave my name to an associate, I make a note of it. In each issue of my newsletter, I list everyone who gave me a referral—even if it didn't turn into an actual project. If a referral does become a client, the person who initiated the contact receives a 10-percent-off certificate for their next invoice and a Pez™ candy dispenser with a label on it that says "Thanks for passing my name along. When we work together, anything is Pez™-able!" I have been in many of my clients' offices and found the Pez™ dispenser sitting on top of their desks, constantly reminding them about me.

A bonus I never expected is that occasionally clients return the discount certificate with a note that says, "You're worth whatever you charge. No discount needed." I don't need to explain what a great feeling that brings!

> Dana Burke is the founder of Mind Your Business, providing desktop publishing services and marketing communications for micro businesses and small non-profits. She also publishes Barefoot Marketing, a free newsletter on marketing your company. Dana has been featured in many publications including *USA Today*, *Success* Magazine, *Business Start-Ups* Magazine and a variety of websites. Dana can be reached at 414-536-7274 or by email at DBurke@execpc.com.

Luck is a residue of your own design.
You create your own luck by acting upon
the opportunities that come your way.
Everyone has the opportunity to be lucky.

—Debbie Allen

Chapter Five

Give It Away

I owe my success to having listened respectfully to the very best advice, and then going away and doing the exact opposite.

—G.K. Chesterton

Shameless Self Promotion Step 5: Stay Active in Your Community by Networking and Volunteering

Debbie Allen

In 1990 I sold my first two retail women's apparel stores in Indiana and moved for a much warmer lifestyle to Scottsdale, Arizona. When I got there I thought I would take a year off, relax, and enjoy myself before opening another store. However, an idle mind and too much time on my hands just doesn't work for me. Within a matter of months, I was already opening my third retail store.

Not knowing anyone in my new hometown, I realized that getting involved in the community was the quickest and least expensive way for me to build my business. I joined eight different networking organizations and volunteered in many of them. I joined Toastmasters to hone my speaking skills and build my confidence. (I bet those of you who know me today find it hard to believe I was ever shy or felt ill at ease in a crowd, but I did.)

I recommend Toastmasters to anyone who plans to be a successful self promoter. Not only will it build your confidence, it will give you a testing ground to network and meet new customers. The speaking skills you learn will help you improve your image when you speak before a group and support your self promotion.

Networking in community organizations led me to meet new customers and many savvy businesswomen. Among them I looked for opportunities to build stronger working relationships. Some of the best opportunities came from the salon owners I met. We all had the same customer base but were in no competition with one another. I knew there was a strong alliance available here. I offered to present fashion seminars and informal fashion shows inside their salons. The salon owners loved the idea and even offered to pay all the expenses to host the event. They invited their best customers, catered the event, and filled the room with women thirsty to learn how to dress better—my customer base! I showed up, entertained, informed, and showcased my business. There was no expense to me, except for my time. I walked away with new friends, new customers, and name recognition for my retail store. The attendees had a great time and felt appreciated. And the salon owners gained customers for life. It was a win-win for everyone involved.

Everyone has information to share with others. What can you speak about that will help others and promote your business at the same time? What strategic alliance can you create to make this happen for you and your business? What other businesses have the same customer base that could benefit from your services? The rewards and opportunities are endless!

Time to Give Back

Mark Victor Hansen

I was bankrupt and upside down when I started selling my speaking services 26 years ago. I met a couple of big name speakers who offered to mentor me and help me out. They stated that if I was willing to put out the effort to sell the seminars they would help me put them together. I went knocking on ten doors a day to sell my seminars for just $25 each. Most of the time I was turned down, but I finally got some takers and spoke for breakfast, lunch, and dinner meetings wherever I could. Now my speaking fee is $20,000, and my goal is to raise it to $100,000.

When I started out in my speaking career I didn't know how I was going to do it. But I knew that if I got people to hire me I would figure it out. I teach the opposite of what they do at Toastmasters. I say "Sell it first, and then figure out how to do it." When someone is paying you, you have real motivation to figure out how to do it. I still do that. I sell stuff, offer big promises (just like in advertising), and then go figure out how to produce, practice, and make it work.

Speakers who come to me with their hard luck stories about how there are not enough talks are wrong! There is no lack of *talk*, there is a lack of people doing marketing. Most people won't do the right marketing to keep stuff going, but there is no lack of business and planning. The world never needed speakers more. My goal is to find and train 1,000 superstar speakers so that the whole world can hear their messages. If the speakers were to divide up the world's population and talk to everyone over a lifetime everyone would be inspired.

I have been very blessed to grow up in an industry that is great. Jack and I now give back at every level. Last year seven co-authors from our *Chicken Soup for the Soul*™ series became millionaires. In addition, every one of our books is tied into a charity. The world needs help and we want to make a difference! One of the reasons you get rich is so you can afford to help charities and help others. On top of that you get a whole level of publicity and promotion. At that level you have so much publicity that it chases you instead of your going after it. All because you want to make a difference and help give back to people in the process.

Mark Victor Hansen, Certified Speaking Professional, is co-creator of the Chicken Soup for the Soul™ series. This series has sold more self-help books than any other in history, 68 million copies. Mark presents high-energy, entertaining programs in the area of business motivation and sales. Mark's office can be contacted at 800-433-2314 or view his website to download one of his books for free at www.MarkVictorHansen.com.

Sell More by Giving Things Away

Don Cooper

The most powerful four-letter word in marketing is "free." Here are two stories recently shared with us that illustrate how guerrillas capitalize on this principle.

Story 1: A Golden Prospecting Opportunity

Guerrillas look for an edge when they prospect—something unusual, creative, or unexpected that will help them stand out from the crowd. Rick Hines, Sales Manager for George Fischer, Inc., recently discovered a tactic worth its weight in gold.

"I had received one of those new dollar coins, the golden colored ones, and while I was visiting a prospect, I asked her, 'Hey, have you seen the new golden dollar?' I took it out of my pocket and showed it to her. She was so intrigued, I told her to go ahead and keep it. Then she really got excited!

"I immediately went to the bank and bought 20 more golden dollar coins. Each time I give one to a prospect, the reaction is the same—amazement, excitement, and tremendous appreciation. It's a small gift; after all, it's only a dollar, but it has a huge impact."

What makes this such a powerful tactic is that people love to be among the *first* to see and experience new things: the latest techno-gadget, a new sports car, or your latest product offering. It makes them feel special. And because you're the one who's making it possible, you become special to them.

Story 2: Free Puppies

A pet shop owner puts up a big sign in his shop: "Free Puppies." Naturally, after people pick out their free puppy, they need to buy puppy food, a puppy bed, puppy dishes, puppy treats, puppy toys, puppy leashes, and all the rest. Customers typically spend more than a hundred dollars to outfit their new pet.

The pet store owner also has relationships with a veterinarian, a fencing contractor, an obedience school teacher, and a cleaning service owner.

Each refers business to the others and helps up-sell the customer: the vet recommends premium dog food; the obedience school recommends more frequent house cleanings during shedding season. And it all starts by giving away a puppy.

What can *you* give away to encourage people to buy from you? Here are 16 good ideas:

Samples
Accessories
Gift certificates
T-shirts
Hats
Ad specialties—pens, notepads, coffee mugs, calendars, etc.
Community service
Refreshments
Consultations
Bumper stickers
Event tickets
Candy
Pre-paid calling cards
Lottery tickets
Buttons and pins
Referrals

Because we practice what we teach, you can get a free audio cassette filled with more guerrilla sales tactics. Just call 800-247-9145 or email Don@GuerrillaGroup.com. And you will find free articles and tips for increasing your sales at www.GuerrillaGroup.com.

> Don Cooper is a partner in The Guerrilla Group, Inc., an international training and consulting firm that helps companies radically increase their sales. For more information, call 800-247-9145 or view the website at www.GuerrillaGroup.com.

Reverse Shoplifting

Greg Godek

When I go into a bookstore and do not see my book it really bothers me. So I created what I call "reverse shoplifting." I give the bookstore a book for free—without telling them!

Here's how it works: I go into the stores that do not carry my book and place my book quietly on the shelf when no one is looking. Eventually someone will want to buy the book and will take it to the counter to pay for it. The retailer will scan the book and discover that it is not in their inventory. What are they going to say to the customer? "Sorry, we don't carry this book." The customer is going to come back with "Yes you do, here it is, and I want to buy it!" Now, any smart retailer is going to make a note of this book as "need to order." This is the goal of reverse shoplifting.

When I did it the first time, I felt as if I was really shoplifting because it is kind of sneaky, but it works!

I'm a strong believer in building your business by giving things away. I give away about 6,000 books a year. When I do radio interviews, I give away ten books instead of just one or two. I can afford to do this because I'm self-published and buy my books in large quantities.

Most people don't think about the actual expense of giving things away as a low-cost marketing strategy. They think only about the retail price of the product. So, if this is the way you think, start to change your mindset. You will then start to reap the rewards of an effective marketing tool: Giving Things Away. People love to get something for FREE. At the same time it will be building a stronger relationship between you and your customer.

> Greg Godek is the author of the best-selling *1001 Ways to Be Romantic* (1.7 million copies sold). Greg is a consultant who works with authors who want to be bestsellers. He also presents romance seminars in his spare time. Contact Greg at 858-456-7177 or find out more about his book and/or seminars at www.Godek.com.

From Flyers to the Internet

Susan Levin

When I started my speaker services business I recognized that professional people could use speaking as part of their marketing plan. These professionals didn't have any place to go to get bookings to promote their business. Speakers' bureaus only book professional paid speakers, but there was nothing out there for professionals who speak to promote their businesses.

You are an expert in your field with a lot of information to share, so why not get out in front of an audience to promote your products and/or services. If you need help in speaking, hire a coach. Or train yourself by getting your hands on as many books and tapes that relate to speaking as possible. Start listening to as many speakers as you can to keep you motivated and informed.

I started out with a print directory that featured speakers for free. It took off right away. Before long we were distributing about 25,000 copies through the mail and on the streets. That became my first marketing tool that people held onto for years.

A couple of years later I got my business onto the Internet. I couldn't wait to stop the printing and put this information on the Web. Now my business has become international and I promote speakers for "free" and professional speakers for "fee."

Some of my best marketing has been on the Internet and with the use of email. I love email because it costs virtually nothing. A lot of people don't realize how valuable a tool it is, and when you discover how valuable it can be, you too will be amazed. You can use email to stay in contact with your customers by sending monthly tips, an electronic newsletter, and/or market your products and/or services on your website.

I send out two or three emails a week. Not all of these are promoting my business. I give out free information as well so that people look forward to reading my email. Giving information for free not only helps others, it's a great way to market yourself. You will be keeping your name out there for the world to see.

Be very generous with information; always be there for people. I don't believe there is competition, but that there is enough to go around for everybody. People are always amazed how much information I will share with them, yet it always comes back around!

> Susan Levin is a publisher, speaker, seminar leader, and marketing consultant for speakers. Susan has owned and created businesses ranging from a health food store, a clothing line, a singles' organization, lecture series and symposiums, and a magazine publisher. Her current business is a web-based directory that supports professional people in growing their business through speaking. Contact Susan at 310-822-4922 or view her website at www.speakerservices.com.

Try Giving Yourself Away

Jean Desmond

Try Giving Yourself Away was the title of a book I read as a young woman. Luckily titles cannot be copyrighted because this one is so appropriate to my topic of self promotion that I can't resist using it. Remember: self promotion is not spelled S-E-L-F-I-S-H. The best way to become known is to help other people in their own endeavors. You needn't do that in a calculating fashion.

Join groups with interests similar to yours: trade organizations, writers' groups, Toastmasters, chambers of commerce, fraternal clubs such as the Lions…anywhere you can meet and network with people seeking success in your field. Then get active. Don't sit in the audience and think, "Okay, what's in this for me?" It's a well-known fact that in every group, 20 percent of the members do 80 percent of the work. Be one of that 20 percent! Volunteer for every job that fits your talents. Get known as a doer, someone to be depended on in a pinch. Run for office; many organizations have a problem finding members willing to serve. Contribute your ideas to their newsletter. And have fun doing it!

In my long career (I'm 81) I have been a model in New York City; a retailer on Madison Avenue; area manager for Weight Watchers in Australia, New Zealand and Brazil; a sales rep selling sexy lingerie on the West Coast; and, finally, a self-published writer. Although I never took a course in public relations, I've learned a lot along the way about what works and what doesn't!

As a free-lance model in the 1940s and 1950s, I sent out brochures to any company that might use my services. Including a photo of me in a swimsuit, I listed my measurements and experience (in the beginning I had to invent the latter). Before each trade show, I mailed several hundred, first class postage. After a while business was so good that I didn't have to advertise to get work.

I entered every beauty contest in the New York area, and occasionally I won. My picture was in the newspapers so often that a friend remarked,

"Every time I wrap up the garbage, there's your photo!" That helped keep my name before the public.

Early in my modeling career a newcomer asked me for advice in finding work. I was telling her how I had started when another girl interrupted. "She's your size and competition to you. Why are you giving away your secrets?"

Another model butted in impatiently, "Oh, there's room for everybody!" That should be your attitude. Do whatever you can to help others; without seeking it, help will come back to you when you need it. Oh sure, once in a while you'll get a kick in the teeth, but that's life. In the long run, friendliness, not rivalry, pays off.

From my experiences as a retailer, I'd advise you to find a niche in your own business—a service not offered by others. When I opened my bra boutique in New York City in the early 1960s, I had to think of something to differentiate me from my competitors. I sent a news release to *Women's Wear Daily* announcing my opening and stating that I planned to fit women who had had breast surgery. The business I got from that kept me solvent.

In protest against the Vietnam War I moved to Sydney in 1970. Having eaten my way across Europe and gained 28 pounds, I joined then fledgling Weight Watchers. I lost the weight and then trained to be a leader, figuring that was the best way to prevent gaining it back. I was asked to train other leaders and opened offices that quickly beat all but one franchise in the entire world.

I ran free rallies in theaters and presented luncheons to show how people could eat well and lose weight on the Weight Watchers program. Inviting newspaper reporters, government officials, and others, we got tremendous publicity in the print media and on TV.

Next I took on the biggest challenge of my life. In partnership with Weight Watchers International, I established the organization in Rio de Janeiro, Brazil, where it is thriving still.

Besides writing about what you know, read! Some of the best self-help books are Dale Carnegie's *How to Win Friends and Influence People*; Napoleon Hill's *Think and Grow Rich*; and David Schwartz's *the Magic of*

Thinking Big. Listen to "success" tapes while driving. Invest money in your education; it will pay off for the rest of your life.

My final career is as an author. I wrote *Look Back and Laugh: Confessions of a Teen in the Thirties* while living in Rio in 1976. It was too scandalous to publish while I needed to earn a living, so I decided to self publish it. Rereading my book as I put it on my computer, I realized how, in my youth, no one would help me escape the slums of New York. They ridiculed my ambition and denigrated my dreams. Luckily as I grew older, many people came to my aid and helped me become successful in almost every endeavor. Perhaps that is the reason I enjoy helping others. Now I'm working with a publicist to become internationally famous—at 81! I'm looking forward to going out with a bang when I'm 100.

> Jean Desmond, a child of the Depression, by age 11 was selling the Saturday Evening Post on the streets of Brooklyn, New York, to help support her family. She tells the story of her first 20 years in her book, *Look Back and Laugh: Confessions of a Teen in the Thirties* and is currently working on her second memoir, *My Side of the Story*. At 81, she plans two more books to bring her to age 100. You can contact Jean at 310-544-1278 or view her website at www.JeanDesmond.com.

Giving It Away to Attract Buyers

Doug Smart

I've had lots of jobs, but two careers. My first career was in the real estate business and I developed it to the point I owned a brokerage in New Orleans. Because many of the people I hired became discouraged by the slow, hard work it took to build a solid client base, I led weekly sales meetings that were motivational and humorous. They were popular, we were successful, and I had a lot of fun. I found it deeply satisfying to stand in front of groups of people and offer them help, hope, and humor.

Later, I sold the company and worked for a few years at a job that eventually became stifling. By the time I turned 36 I had run low on money and realized I wanted to be self-employed again. This lead to my second career. I didn't immediately know what kind of work to do or how to transition into it. Fortunately, I happened to come across a book on starting a speaking business, an opportunity that sounded custom-made for me. The book was packed with practical ideas, such as "Offer a free seminar so new clients can test-drive you."

This was a bold way to advertise that didn't cost me any money. And it gave me a way to find out what reactions people in different industries would have to me as a speaker. Following the advice in the book, I mailed letters to 50 training directors who worked for the largest employers in New Orleans. I offered each a free one-hour seminar for a small group of their employees. The topic was "How to Handle Difficult People," as I figured that subject was universally appealing. I said in my letter that I was a professional speaker looking to expand my business. I added that as compensation, I wanted a letter of reference if they liked my presentation. In addition, I hoped they would consider hiring my company (which only existed in my mind) to present future training. Eight directors, including the person in charge of employee education at the mammoth New Orleans Hilton, said, "Yes." This was wonderful and terrifying—wonderful because they saw enough value to take a chance on me, yet terrifying because I had neither a company nor a seminar.

I was nervous. I spent hours in agony as I wrote and rewrote a script. For the Hilton, I gamely presented a seminar for 60 employees in the housekeeping department. Stammering, stuttering, and bungling through, I served up a lively program that addressed some of the real challenges they faced. They participated in the group activities and laughed a lot. Compared to professional speakers, I was amateurish, but my heart was in the right place. The training director and the audience members knew I cared about their success.

When I asked for a testimonial letter, the training director wrote a gushy one on beautiful Hilton letterhead that praised how delightful I was to work with and stated, "Afterwards, everyone was talking about you in the hallways." (Yeah, I bet they were!) "You said things to us that no one has ever said before." (I'm afraid I did!) Though she may have written it partially tongue-in-cheek, I proudly flashed that letter around to potential clients and proclaimed, "Look what I did for the Hilton! I can do this for you, too!"

The other seven (representing Tulane University Medical Center, Louisiana State University Medical Center, Louisiana Power and Light, the City of New Orleans, and others) also wrote brief letters of glorious overblown praise. The referral letters helped me to quickly gain the toehold I needed to start my new career. I was not shy about showing those impressive letters to potential clients! A few months later they caught the attention of a national training company which hired me to lead 150 seminars the following year —and that proved to me I would make it as a motivational speaker.

I attribute my quick-start success to something I learned in the beginning and still practice today: Giving away the product is sometimes the best way to attract buyers.

> Doug Smart has delivered over 1,000 seminars around the world. He hosts a daily radio show, "Smarter by the Minute," with over 300,000 listeners each week. He has authored or co-authored seven books. Contact Doug at 770-587-9784 or view his website at www.DougSmart.com.

When you are forgotten, you cease to exist!

—The Lady of the Lake in the TV special "Merlin"
(contributed by Larry James)

Chapter Six

Your Expertise Is Showing

*The higher up you go,
the more mistakes you're allowed.
When at the top, if you make enough of them,
it's considered to be your style.*

—Fred Astaire

Self Promotion Step 6:
Take Your Expertise to Another Level

Debbie Allen

After a few years of sharing my expertise in public seminars and emceeing fashion shows to promote my business, I became hooked on speaking. My form of self promotion was actually helping people. I felt as if I was changing lives, even at some small level. I dreamed of someday speaking professionally about my true loves—business and marketing. I wanted to make a difference on a much larger scale.

I shared my dream with a friend and sales associate, Stuart Marks. "You would be great! I know the person who manages this tradeshow, we've been friends for years. I bet he would be interested in having you speak here at the next show," said Stuart. "His name is Roland Timney. In fact, I'll give him a call right now."

I had five minutes to come up with a seminar title, a sales pitch, and a fee. Roland loved the idea of having seminars at the show and even agreed to pay me $1,000. plus travel expenses.

Wow, what a great start! I had made it! That was easy! I couldn't wait to tell all my friends and family that I was going to be a professional speaker and that I had my first paid engagement. Or so I thought!

A month went by and Roland had not returned my phone calls to confirm the booking. Why would he not be calling me back? I started to worry about the prospect and finally called my friend and newfound agent, Stuart, for some help and support. I asked Stuart if he could call Roland and see why he was not returning my calls. Within 30 minutes the phone rang and Roland was on the other end. "Sorry I haven't called you back," said Roland. I'm thinking, No problem, I'm sure he had been too busy to call me back, but now we are going to close the deal. "Debbie, I haven't called you back because the moneyman does not believe that seminars are going to get more attendees to the show. He's just not going for it. Of course, I believe differently, I know that you have a lot of knowledge and expertise to share. You could really help these retailers and build up the attendance at our tradeshow. But, sorry we can't do it!"

I sat at my desk broken and defeated. I felt like crawling under a rock and never coming out to face the world again. After all, I had already told everyone I knew that I was going to be a professional speaker. This was my big break! Suddenly, all my hopes and dreams had faded.

Or so I thought! After five minutes of wallowing in my own personal pity party, I snapped out of it. *Wait a minute; there is still an opportunity here. I just need to figure out a way to make it happen! There must be a way. Let me think.* Roland said he believed in the seminar and my expertise, so I forced myself not to take his rejection personally. He said it was the moneyman. That means that they don't have a budget for speakers. Now, I can't do this for free because I'm trying to get professional, paid seminars. I tried to think of another way I could make it happen and have everyone benefit from it?

For the next couple of hours I focused in on what I really wanted to accomplish from this seminar. What was more important than the money? Exposure! That's what I really needed. I needed to showcase my talents and expertise so that more people would hire me to speak.

I wanted to call Roland back right then and say, "I'll do it for free!" Instead, I forced myself to sleep on it and come up with an even better plan.

My Plan

The next morning I called Roland with a new option. I told him, "I know you believe that seminars are needed to motivate and inform the attendees of your show. And again, I appreciate the trust you have instilled in me to accomplish this. I also understand that you do not have a budget for speakers. So, in order to make it a win-win situation for everyone, I'll do the seminar free if you agree to pay all of my travel expenses."

The bottomline for me was that I was ahead of the game just by asking for the travel expenses. I needed to attend the show anyway, to buy merchandise for my store, and I wanted the added exposure that attending the show would give me.

However, I had come up with more. "I also ask that you promote me and my seminar in all of your marketing materials." This included thousands of direct mail pieces, the front cover of the show newspaper, and a huge poster in the lobby. If I did a great job, I was sure I could get a testimonial letter. I knew that the publicity from the show would give me thousands of dollars worth of exposure and that was what I needed most at this point in my new career. I also knew that they had already planned to pay for marketing materials to get attendees to the show. By adding my seminar it gave the mailer an added benefit and did not cost them anything more.

Roland went for my new plan. Great, now I had to prepare the seminar. It took months. I knew I had to make the most of this opportunity. I asked Roland to put me on for the second day of the tradeshow so that I could help to promote the event while at the show.

I brought in some shameless self promotion when I asked my sales associates to help be my promoters as well. They told every customer that came to their booths about my seminar and how it would help grow their business to another level of success. I did my own share of self promotion, starting with the shuttle bus ride to the shows. By the time the bus had arrived at the show, I had a captive audience excited about attending.

The Big Day Arrives

The seminar room was packed with business owners, managers and a few supportive sales associates. I was thrilled at the great turnout, but scared to speak before this savvy group of business owners. I held my composure well, however, even when the plug on my projector got pulled and I lost all of my slides. Looking behind me, I saw one of my sales associates crawling on his hands and knees across the floor to fix the connection. "Ignore the man behind the curtain," I said, and everyone laughed. I included other references to the "the crawling man," using it to explain my message of the value of working, supporting, and learning from one another when growing your business to another level of success.

The event was a hit, the first in a series of many successful seminars at this show. Roland gave me one of the best testimonial letters I have ever received. In fact, it is still part of my portfolio and appears on my website today. Thank you, Roland and Stuart, for your belief in my expertise and for helping to jumpstart my dream career!

Secrets of a Modest Success

Ron Arden

We've all heard the expression, "Word of mouth is the best form of advertising." (That's other people's mouths, of course.) That may be true, but it's also the slowest form.

To get known quickly, self promotion is an accepted part of advertising. However, for it to be speedily effective it has to be assertive. If it's too modest and quiet-spoken, there's a good chance nobody's going to notice. Hence, the wellworn cliche, "If you don't blow your own horn, nobody's going to blow it for you" holds more than a germ of truth.

This is where shameless self promotion comes in. If you're like me, the idea of shameless self promotion causes you to break into an instant sweat. "It's too hard for me," I think. "I can't do it." I don't shy from extolling my virtues, but it's the "shameless" part that makes me flinch.

When shameless self promotion is done well it works well, but not everyone is equipped to do it. I know I'm not. I am without a doubt the worst self promoter in the world. I've never had a brochure, never done any advertising, am too British to call people and sell my services. I sweat for hours trying to write a squib about myself. I'm embarrassed having to call a client to remind them of a long-booked appointment. I agonize when I want to increase my fees. In the conventional marketing sense I have always hidden my light under a bushel.

However, once I'm onstage, whether it's in front of an audience or talking to one of my current or potential clients, my reticence melts away and I'm firm, to the point of being arrogant, about my beliefs and opinions.

So, what is the secret of my modest success? Being there at the right time and knowing it's the right time and right for me. Being good at what I do and being fairly intense in declaring it. Being contrary and provocative whenever the opportunity presents itself so people will remember me.

Showing openly that I love what I do so people will recognize my sincerity. And, I am told, I possess a teeny sliver of charm.

The critical element that must never be left out of this equation is that when you sound off, you had better be right much more than you're wrong. And you've got to have charm. Charm makes the whole mix palatable.

So, shamelessly promote your virtues and shamelessly hide your vices but never forget there are other ways. They hold more good taste, more dignity, more style, more class, and more elegance, but, unless you're extraordinarily lucky, as I am, without shameless self promotion there's a chance you may not be able to stay in business long enough to enjoy them.

> Ron Arden is widely regarded as the guru of coaches to the speaking profession. His clientele includes such greats as Ken Blanchard, Mark Victor Hansen, Ty Boyd, and Brian Tracy. Ron can be reached at 619-222-1499 or by email at RonArden@aol.com.

Starting Over

Karen Lawson

Like many women in the middle and late sixties, I had my life all planned. To a great degree, it was pretty much planned for me. First of all, I was limited (or thought I was limited) to becoming a teacher, nurse, or secretary. So, with some prodding from my parents I decided to be a teacher, because as my mother said, "Teaching is a good job for a woman."

So off to college I went with this plan: get an education, marry Prince Charming, teach a couple years, quit to have children, and then go back to work when the children go to school. Sounds like a good plan, right? Well, things didn't quite turn out as expected. I got my degree, got married, and started teaching. However, my prince turned out to be a frog and my perfect plan disappeared in a puff of smoke, but not before I had tried to hang onto the fairy tale for 12 years.

I used to think success was having money, fame, recognition, and being Mrs. Somebody. After the marriage fell apart, I wasted days, weeks, and months feeling sorry for myself and bemoaning my fate. If I had just been born to different parents, grown up in a different town, or married the right man. I became angry, bitter, and envious of others who seemed to have it all. I focused only on the poor choices and mistakes I had made.

Then one day I decided to change my life and the way I viewed myself. I'm not sure when my wake-up call came, but I do remember the process I followed. I began by deciding who I wanted to be. Then I looked at who I was and quickly concluded that the real and ideal were pretty far apart. I went through a painful process of self-discovery and analysis to identify the reasons why I was not as effective in my relationships—personally and professionally—as I wanted to be and knew I could be. I then embarked on a plan of self-improvement that included seeking and receiving feedback from others, becoming more positive about life in general, and consciously replacing negative behaviors with positive ways of interacting with others. It's been a long, but rewarding journey, once I identified and focused on the four P's of success: purpose, perseverance, personal power, and passion.

Purpose

The first thing you need to be successful is a purpose. You need to set both short- and long-term goals. Studies show that the most successful people in the world set goals, then establish and follow a game plan to meet those goals.

I started doing some serious goal setting in 1991. I had been toying with the idea of going back to school to get my doctorate, but I was afraid. After all, it had been a long time since I had been in school. I mentioned my concern to a friend and told her that I was hesitant because I would be 50 by the time I finished. She said, "So what? You're going to be 50 anyway. Do you want to be 50 with a PhD or without one?" What a great question! So I decided to set three major goals. By the time I turned 50, I planned to have my PhD, CSP (Certified Speaking Professional, an earned designation from the National Speakers Association), and have a book published. And I'm proud to say that I met all three goals a year early.

Perseverance

The second "P" is perseverance. Never give up on yourself or your dreams. At the same time, you must be flexible and learn to adapt to changing circumstances. The ability to bounce back is critical to success.

I left the corporate world and the security of a steady paycheck in 1986 and started my own business in Rochester, New York. When I moved to Philadelphia with husband number two in 1989, I knew no one and no one knew me. I don't know if I expected some great announcement that Karen Lawson was in town and that the calls would start streaming in, but they didn't. So I decided I had better get connected with the professional community.

We had only been in the area two weeks, and I drove myself down to Center City to attend a meeting. I picked up my nametag, took a deep breath, and walked into the meeting room. There were several clusters of people gathered, so I got up the courage to walk up to one group and introduce myself: "Hi, I'm Karen Lawson. I've only been in the area two weeks, and I'm really excited about joining this chapter." They stopped and turned toward me. One person said, "How nice," and then they all turned away and continued their conversation. I can take a hint, so I tried my luck with another cluster. Similar response. I was beginning to wonder if I had forgotten to use deodorant or mouthwash. So I retreated to a corner of the room and prayed for the meeting to start. I was upset, but concluded that I just happened to pick the wrong groups.

So I went back the next month and the same thing happened. When I went home that night I told my husband that I would give them one more chance, and if I was treated the same way, I would never go back. As luck would have it, at the third meeting, I sat next to the president who couldn't have been nicer. She made me feel warm and welcome and invited me to join a committee.

That was only the beginning. For the next few years, I practically made a career of going to meetings, working on committees, giving free speeches and seminars—anything to establish my credibility and gain name recognition. I wrote articles for trade publications and newsletters, spoke at conventions and conferences for free, and I networked like crazy.

There were many times that I wanted to give up. I can remember several times when I walked away from a training program or speaking engagement feeling like a failure and vowing to find another way to make a living.

I also came close to giving up on getting my PhD. Shortly after I started working on my doctorate, my husband was outplaced as a result of downsizing, rightsizing—whatever you want to call it—from a large corporation where he had worked for 23 years. During the following two years, things were tough. I was going to school and trying to restart my business in a new area. So many times I was tempted to give up on the idea of having my own consulting business, get a real job, and forget about the PhD. In fact, I even received a couple of offers for internal training positions, but I couldn't do it.

No matter how tough it was, I was convinced that I could make a go of the business, and I was determined not to give up. This experience with Bob's outplacement brings me to the third "P": Personal Power.

Personal Power

As the months dragged on and Bob was still unemployed, I began to understand what it's like to have others depend on you for food and shelter. I became more driven to get more speaking engagements and training contracts. I panicked with every cancellation or postponement. I began to feel what many single parents and sole providers must feel: the anxiety, pressure, and fear of losing your job.

What I really learned from that experience is empathy. I learned that empathy along with compassion and understanding are the keys to personal power and influence.

Personal power is not only the ability to empathize but also the ability to influence, that is, to be a compelling force on the thoughts, opinions, and behavior of others. This ability to influence others is truly an art. Although it employs a variety of skills, influencing draws primarily on our ability to understand others and ourselves.

Just as the artist starts with a vision when he or she sees a blank canvas or a lump of clay, we as individuals have a picture in our minds of who we are, who we want to be, and how we want to relate to and interact with others. To bring his or her vision to life, a painter decides the proper mix of colors, pulling just the right amount of color from each of the daubs on the palette. In a similar fashion, we must decide on the appropriate mix of strategies and behaviors to achieve our desired results.

Passion

The artist creates a masterpiece spawned by his or her burning passion for truth and beauty and an uncontrollable desire to express it. We, too, can express our passion for life and for those around us. Without passion, life is merely a series of experiences. Pursue your passion, and you will find success.

Each one of us must define success for ourselves, not benchmark against someone else or some ideal image of what success looks or feels like. As Katherine Graham once said, "To love what you do and feel that it matters—how could anything be more fun?"

> Karen Lawson, PhD and Certified Speaking Professional, inspires, involves, and informs her audiences on leadership, influence, team development, and communications. She is the author of Involving Your Audience. Karen can be contacted at 215-368-9465 or view her website at www.LawsonCG.com.

Reaching Emerging Markets

Lenora Billings-Harris

Robert, Faheem, Tracee, Kewal, Lois, Hernando, and Dorothy are account executives for a small but rapidly growing company. Their ages range from 23 to 59 years old; two are single, two are married, two have domestic life partners; three are child-free, three are parents; one is gay and one is blind; one is caring for a parent and two children; two are single parents. There are four languages and six religious faiths represented by this group. This is diversity!

The word "diversity" simply means differences or variety. As used when referring to the American workplace and market, diversity refers to the many differences present among people today that were not recognized in large numbers in the past.

The marketplace for all products and services is growing at warp speed. Are you taking advantage of the great opportunities to expand your business success within emerging Asian, Hispanic, African-American and women's markets? Regardless of what product or service you offer, no longer is it enough to be an expert in your field. The most successful businesses and entrepreneurs recognize that they must also understand today's diverse markets, and utilize creative marketing strategies and techniques to connect with them.

Therefore, it is important to build your knowledge and understanding of different groups, so that you do not rely on biases or stereotypes that exist due to lack of information. Additionally, you don't want to offend people simply because you were not aware of multicultural behaviors. For example, the American "bye-bye" gesture means "come here" to some people from Southeast Asia. Some Koreans can interpret smiling during business transactions as frivolous behavior. Do your homework by conducting research on the Internet, talking to people in the group you wish to reach, and by getting involved in organizations whose members are representative of the group with whom you wish to do business. You will then be building on your diversified marketing knowledge and expertise!

The most effective marketing techniques help you build a lasting relationship with your prospects and clients. This is especially true for emerging markets. Your clients are interested in knowing whether you are interested in them as people or if you just want their dollars. Developing relationships is a long-term process, and it has big pay-offs.

Suggestions for Promotion to Emerging Markets

▼ Sponsor/support athletic and student group events (e.g., ethnic sororities and fraternities).

▼ Join specialized chambers of commerce: African-American, Hispanic, Asian, and women.

▼ Create an award/list patterned after the Fortune 500 lists that relate to your product or service. Example: America's 50 Best Companies for Minorities. Develop processes for nominations and selection, including a media event to announce the winner.

Lenora Billings-Harris, Certified Speaking Professional, is the author of *The Diversity Advantage* and *A Guide to Making Diversity Work*. To learn more about Lenora's diversity training and/or her books contact her at 888-288-8885 or view her website at www.LenoraSpeaks.com.

Sell Yourself and the $$$ Come Easy

Fred Berns

Self promotion doesn't just make sense. It makes money. You can substantially increase the fees that you set and get or the salary you command simply by blowing your horn and tooting your flute. You can set and get any fee or salary you want to as long as you can adequately differentiate yourself from competitors who charge or request less.

"To be successful, you have to be unique," Walt Disney once said. "So different, that if people want what you have, they have to come to you to get it." And, once they do, they'll pay the price—your price.

You must add magic to your message in a way that clearly sets you apart from others who do what you do and want what you want. So, what makes you different?

Present yourself as a specialist. Talk about your special skills, your special area of expertise, and the clients with whom you specialize. Discuss your accomplishments and awards, degrees, and other recognition you've received. Recall former occupations or areas of study.

How well you promote yourself will determine how prosperous you become. Consider the people you need to know in order for you to succeed. Do they know you? Do they appreciate all that you do? All that you have done? All that you can do? If not, is it because you haven't told them? Is that because you don't know?

If you're going to promote yourself up the financial ladder, you must become the world's ultimate information source, the number one authority, and the foremost expert on you. Try keeping a "Winner's Workbook," a daily log of your accomplishments, sales, contributions to your company, recognition you receive, goals you achieve, etc. Compile a list of ten things that make you different, ten "onlys," and ten benefits that those you serve receive from you. That "ammunition" will help you give yourself credit where credit is due, and help convince others of your value.

You can only do the best job of selling yourself by identifying your "only." "Only" is by far the most important word in your self promotion vocabulary. It's the one word that puts you in a class by yourself and best highlights your uniqueness. For example, identify yourself as the only award-winning computer consultant in your area or the firm's only bilingual attorney, and you stand out in ways others do not.

The next step on the road to higher compensation is to present yourself as an "expert." And why not? One of the dictionary definitions of that word is "skilled person." You already are an expert. In the words of talk show host Larry King, "Everyone is an expert on something."

Here's where the courage of your convictions—and your self-esteem—comes into play. There may be only one person holding you back from earning much income. That one person isn't a tough competitor or a difficult customer. That one person is you. Perhaps you haven't given yourself permission to receive the compensation that you want and deserve.

Now's the time to do so. As good as you are at what you do, you deserve to receive lots of money to do it. But, remember, it doesn't matter how good you are if you're the only one who knows. You must sell yourself—all day, everyday. Make that sale—that personal sale, and you'll go from being a wannabe to a winner, from being a striver to an arriver, and from just being busy to earning more money than you ever dreamed possible.

> Fred Berns is a speaker, consultant, and author who helps individuals and organizations dramatically increase profits by promoting themselves more effectively. For more information or to order his book *Sell Yourself!: 501 Ways to Get Them to Buy from You* or other business-building products, contact Fred Berns at 888-665-5505 or view his website at www.FredBerns.com.

Market Yourself as the "Expert"

Irene Levitt

When I first began studying for my masters in handwriting analysis, some of my instructors cautioned me to keep secret how and what I do. They said, "Never tell others the exact way you derive information about their handwriting." That made absolutely no sense to me and, defiantly, when I finished my masters program, the first thing I did was tell others how I do what I do.

I know that handwriting analysis is an empirical science and it seemed irrational not to share my knowledge. My lectures were entertaining but they became teaching sessions as well. It was natural for me to apply to teach at various community colleges, much to the surprise of my speaker colleagues. They often asked why I would want to teach at our local community colleges. They were amazed that I would want to spend so many hours for minimal compensation. Yes, it is true, the college pays very little for my time and expertise. But, in addition to the great pleasure I take in sharing my knowledge with others, I receive many hidden monetary rewards for my efforts.

The college does all my outside marketing for the three handwriting analysis classes I teach every semester. At no charge to me, they direct-mail information about my expertise to all 260,000 citizens in my city. They advertise my classes in the big city newspaper that reaches thousands more who live in nearby cities.

Because of my willingness to teach at the college (and my enthusiastic students), I am stamped as an "expert" in my field. Many large company owners contact me, daily, to assist in hiring personnel. These executives also query the college administrator about my background. They feel comfortable once the college has given me their stamp of approval. Meeting planners contact me to speak for their business meetings and conventions. And I spend not one penny of my own for advertising! Such a deal!

Irene Levitt, MGA, is a music therapist and international speaker and she has a master's degree in graphoanalysis. Her company, Handwriting Consultants, LLC, provides vocational analysis, document examination, criminal investigation, jury screening, personality assessments, and compatibility of business and love relationships. She is the author of four books and an audiotape on handwriting analysis. Irene can be reached at 480-661-9199 or by email at www.Irenelevitt.com.

A Steady Approach

Dan S. Kennedy

One of the most important things I've discovered about self promotion is that the need for it never diminishes. I've been well-served by the following self-imposed discipline: Do something promotional every single day. To me, marketing and promoting myself is as much a part of my daily routine as (my admittedly little bit of) exercising, taking my vitamins, reading the newspaper. This is quite contrary to most peoples' approach, which is to pay attention to self promotion in spurts, often only when waning sales mandate or some opportunity drops from the sky. So, my rule is not to go to sleep at night until I've met my daily self promotion minimum. Some days it might really be minimal: making one phone call, dashing off one note to a media contact. Others ideas include: doing a radio or taped interview, writing an article, getting an email blast out to everyone who has visited my website. But I always do at least one thing.

Here is another of my most important discoveries: the vital need to retell your entire sales story every time you go to your marketplace, constituency, or even your own, most responsive customers. It's natural to assume that your customers know all about your credentials, expertise, experience, and attributes and do not need to hear about all that for the umpteenth time. It is even natural to assume they may tire of hearing about it. But I can assure you that marketing results, including valid split-tests (i.e., carefully testing one variable against another; for example, two different prices or two different headlines) prove this assumption wrong—and costly—and demonstrate the importance of retelling your whole, best story each and every time.

It's also dangerous to tire of telling your own story. I personally fight this from time to time. In a speech or sitting down to write a sales letter to my own customers, I find myself shortcutting the "why you should pay attention to my advice" part of the sales story only because I'm tired of telling it. When I catch myself, I dig in and find yet one more way to organize and deliver that information in an interesting and persuasive way.

It may not be as obvious for the veterinarian or clothing store owner or restaurant owner or you-name-it, but obvious or not, it's just as important.

It is very beneficial to develop expert status and celebrity status within your particular market.

The third of the three most important things I've learned about self promotion is that we tend to gloss over certain facts about our expertise or knowledge that we feel are not worthy of recognition or emphasis. Yet these facts are usually important, intriguing, and persuasive to others. In my book No Rules, I talk about the super sports agent Mark McCormack, and his revealing statement: "Many companies fail to place a premium on the real dollar worth of their expertise." He goes on to describe a vast and valuable body of knowledge he acquired in working with over 1,000 companies on promotions involving athletes and celebrities. He took this experience for granted and gave it away for free for too many years, later realizing it not only had value in real dollars, but was actually his most useful tool for attracting new corporate clients.

Similarly, I find most people fail to place proper premium on their experience, knowledge, and strengths, and too often fail to make maximum use of everything they possess for self promotion.

Even experiences based on past tragedy or disappointment may have present-day value. For example, I often mention in my speeches that, early in my career, I stumbled badly, went through both personal and corporate bankruptcy, started over from scratch, and had to make up lost time and money to create wealth and success. Every single time I've ever mentioned that—and I've done so in most of the nearly 2,000 speeches I've delivered—people have come to me afterward to tell me that in revealing that, I inspired them. They had had similar experiences and were encouraged by mine. They tell me that my "nudge" pushed them over the edge into investing in my resources. Early, quickly, I learned from that, and as a result, have often made a point of talking about this in my literature and in sales letters for my highest-priced boot camps for entrepreneurs. I take the position that there is more to learn from somebody who has failed as well as succeeded.

I've worked with many clients developing comprehensive self marketing, including some celebrities. I helped Joan Rivers develop her material on recovery from tragedy, career success, and happiness that has provided the basis for two of her books, an audio program, and speeches. I helped Rod Smith, a former NFL pro, develop marketing for his non-profit organization's character building summer youth camps. In every case, whether working with a celebrity, a non-famous person, or a corporation, I have always uncovered a number of strengths, assets, experiences, and expertise that were being taken for granted and not being judged worthy of promotion. Yet they provided real promotional power when properly used.

> Dan S. Kennedy is a direct-marketing consultant. As a highly recognized professional speaker, he addresses over 200,000 people each year, sharing the platform with others such as President George Bush Sr., General Norman Schwarzkopf, Colin Powell, and Zig Ziglar. Dan is the author of *How to Make Millions with Your Ideas* and *No Rules: 21 Giant Lies about Success*. You can reach Dan at 602-997-7707 or view his website at www.DanKennedy.com.

You are one of a kind, therefore,
no one can really predict to what heights you might soar.
Even you will not know until you spread your wings!

—Gil Atkinson

Chapter Seven

Get Out There and Work It

> *I look upon every day to be lost*
> *in which I do not make a new acquaintance.*
>
> —Samuel Johnson

Shameless Self Promotion Step 7:
Build a Strongly Connected Group of Strategic Alliances

Debbie Allen

People often get discouraged with networking because they don't see results right away. They forget that networking takes time, focus, and effort. You need to stay out there and in touch, and you need to use the services of other people that you meet. When you show a sincere interest in and support for their business, it will turn around in business for you.

Networking comes naturally for me today because I truly enjoy helping people grow their businesses. When you feel this way, you first and foremost enjoy getting to know new people and learning their businesses. This is the first step in reaping big rewards with your networking.

The next step is to build a strong, strategic alliance base with these contacts. This means that you keep contacting them from time to time for years to come. Don't ever lose the contact! Keep them in mind when referring business. Talk about them and their business in the community. Support them in any way that you can. This is what will really take your networking efforts to the next level of success. Building a dynamic strategic alliance base is like networking on steroids!

There are so many stories of how networking has helped me grow my businesses. In fact, my businesses would not have survived without the knowledge and support of my many strategic alliances.

Here is just one story that may give you an idea on how networking can best serve you. I once went to a meeting about doing business with the state of Arizona, hosted by the Arizona Procurement Office. When I got there I discovered that

I knew one of the speakers on the program. Joseph Dean is the small business advocate for the state and works in the governor's office. He also writes a Phoenix newspaper column targeted to small business owners. Joe and I had met at a networking organization I belonged to years before. Since then I had written articles for Joe's column and presented a seminar on networking at his business tradeshow.

Even though I had not seen Joe for years, I kept the communication open. I would send him a note from time to time on something he might find helpful or informative, or send a referral his way.

Just before Joe got up to speak I went up to him and shared the news that I had sold my third retail store and had started a new business. He immediately said that someone in his office could use my services. So I handed him five business cards, told him how great it was to see him again, and returned to my seat to listen to his talk.

Joseph Dean, a highly respected person from the governor's office, began to speak about marketing and promoting your business. He spoke about how you could promote yourself and open up opportunities to get business from the state. As he got into his presentation, he began to talk about the benefits of networking. Joe told the large group of over 400 people that only two people had taken the time to talk with him and to share their business cards. The rest of this group had missed an opportunity to network and promote themselves.

What happened next came as a pleasant surprise. Joe held up my business card. "Debbie Allen is not only a marketing expert, she is great at networking. She knows how to make businesses succeed and how to look for marketing opportunities around every corner. You could learn a lot from Debbie," Joe said. He brought me up several more times as he made points in his presentation.

At the end of the presentation a number of people jumped at the chance to hand him their business cards. There was a long line of people behind me as well. They talked to me about their businesses and about hiring me for marketing advise and consulting. I formed many new alliances that day and reaped the rewards of new business.

You can do this, too. Just look for opportunities and place yourself in front of them. Not only will you create some wonderful friendships, you will be building your business with enthusiastic strategic alliances.

Networking Is an Attitude

Deb Haggerty

I am passionate about connecting people. In fact, I call my business Positive Connections®! Like my dad, who never knew a stranger, I view folks I don't know as friends I just haven't met yet. When you have that philosophy, anyone in range of a handshake becomes a potential contact for your network.

In other words, networking can happen anytime in any place with anyone! Several months ago, I was standing in the lobby of a hotel in Charleston waiting for the airport shuttle to arrive. Gazing around the lobby, I spied a woman lifting a beautiful silver and royal blue necklace from a shopping bag and looking at it admiringly. Those are my favorite colors and I exclaimed to her, "My what a pretty necklace!" Five little words! We began one of those hotel lobby conversations we sometimes have with people whom we will never see again. She asked me if I was going to the airport and if so, would I like to share the car she had coming? I gratefully accepted her invitation.

As we were loading our luggage into the car, she chirped to me, "And what do you do?" My spirits plummeted. I was tired from a long trip, I didn't want to go into sales mode, and so I tried to be brief. "I'm a professional speaker, but I wasn't here speaking. I was helping a friend."

"Oh, really?" she exclaimed delightedly. "I come to these conferences looking for speakers for my company!"

My inner voice sighed, *Why now? I'm so tired. I don't want to do this.* We got into the car and as we glided off to the airport, she queried, "What do you speak about?" In a totally negative state of mind, I handed her my business card and mumbled that my speeches were listed on the back. She read down the list of talks and asked, "'Right Person, Right Job,' what's that all about?" At that point I gave up and realized I was getting into the conversation whether I wanted to or not. I explained that many of my consulting clients had been burned in the hiring/firing process, that I had found some objective assessments to use in the process, and that the speech taught a better methodology for hiring employees.

"Really!" she excitedly interrupted. "I have to hire someone next week and I can't afford to make a mistake! Please overnight me the marketing materials for these assessments."

When I got home, I sent her the materials. She liked them and purchased the software and the assessments. Next she hired me to come out and spend two days with her department to facilitate team-building in the group. The day I returned from that engagement, I received a call from another group in the same company asking when I could come back and do the same for them!

Five little words brought me almost two-thirds of my revenues for that year and a new friend and positive relationship—and I wasn't even trying!

1985 marked the year I risked it all and launched Positive Connections, my speaking and consulting business. My first two clients were a company I had worked with while at AT&T. During my tenure at AT&T, I had carefully nurtured the relationships with these two groups. Nurturing means carefully tending, gently handling, and valuing the relationship. Valued relationships are to be cherished and cultivated so that they grow strong and fruitful. Scripture teaches, "For if you give, you will get! Your gift will return to you in full and overflowing measure, pressed down, shaken together to make room for more, and running over. Whatever measure you use to give—large or small—will be used to measure what is given back to you."

Networking is also a process that can be learned and followed assiduously. There are three basic steps to networking: Process, People, and Practice.

The first step is **Process.** As part of the process, answer the following questions:

1. Why am I networking?
2. Who will I be networking with?
3. What am I able to give to the process?
4. What do I hope to gain?
5. When will I network?

Next set goals for networking. Decide on a particular time of day or week when you will proactively network. Set up a system for tracking the contacts you make, whether it be the old standard Rolodex, or one of the new

110

computer-based systems. Prepare the tools of networking: business cards, thank you notes, brochures. Make sure that your materials are professional and reflect you. Remember that you want to make positive connections!

People: Where can we network to meet the people we want to build relationships with?

▼ Chambers of commerce
▼ Social clubs
▼ Churches
▼ Networking groups
▼ Professional associations
▼ PTAs
▼ Charitable organizations
▼ Even hotel lobbies!

Practice: To be successful at networking, practice is critical. First impressions are important, so keep in mind that you only have one opportunity to make a positive first impression. Here are five guidelines to follow that will help make the practice perfect!

1. Keep business cards with you at all times, along with a pen for jotting notes on the cards you receive to help you remember where and why you have them.

2. Have a "TMAY" (Tell Me about Yourself). Practice a short phrase that will enable you to respond professionally and in a manner that will attract interest and lead you into a meaningful conversation.

3. Remember the Three Foot Rule: Anyone within three feet (about the length of a handshake) is a prospect and possible contact for you.

4. Always smile at people: It's contagious!

5. Have fun: You never know when you'll meet a new best friend!

Networking is an attitude; process, place, and practice will enable you to impress people favorably! I always try to be alert and listen to the people around me, to find that key connection! Networking is my passion, my pleasure, and my best sales tool!

> *"Networking is an attitude.*
> *You must always keep in mind those people*
> *to whom you can refer others.*
> *In order to receive the benefits of networking*
> *you must first give."*
>
> —Deb Haggerty,
> as quoted in her book, *The Sales Coach*

Deb Haggerty connects organizations and individuals through positive strategies in communication, human resources, and technology with her company, Positive Connections®. Deb is a co-author of these books, *The Sales Coach*, *The Communication Coach*, and *The Masters Collection*. She can be reached at 407-856-2897 or view her website at www.DebHaggerty.

A Network Is Mandatory for Making It

Susan RoAne

People have relied on whom they know for information or referrals since the beginning of time. We have depended on this exchange of shared resources, time immemorial. Networking is defined by *Webster's Unabridged Encyclopedia Dictionary* as "the act or process of informally sharing information or support, especially among members of a professional group." Networking is a reciprocal process, an exchange of ideas, leads, and suggestions that support both our professional and our personal lives.

There is also a spirit of sharing that transcends the information shared. The best networkers reflect that spirit with a genuine joy in giving. We all have networks we were born into, went to school with, live in neighborhoods with, and work with. Savvy networkers understand that networking is a process of communication that works for those who appreciate the path and process as well as the destination.

One cannot stress enough just how important it is to develop and finely hone follow-up skills. There is no process of networking, no sharing of information, resource, or referral that occurs without it.

Secrets to Savvy Networking

1. Follow-up is a basic tenet of life.

2. Behaviors and actions support words; the lack of either subverts them. We must T.A.P. into our networks, being Timely and Appropriately Persistent in our follow-up, or we will fail to establish and increase our base of contacts. That is networking in a nutshell!

3. People who have resources are resourceful. People who are willing to open their Rolodex™ or contact management program, pick up a phone, call on their contacts, and ask for help and solutions, and who offer leads, information, and ideas, are perceived as powerful and smart. The closest thing to knowing something is to know where and how to find it.

4. Acknowledge gifts given to you as well as leads, ideas, advice and time.

5. Powerful people have linkages that are plentiful, diverse, and expansive, and they are able to get things done because of those linkages. President Clinton's superb and savvy networking skills cannot be denied. He was elected because of his network!

What Are the Special Networking Skills of the Masters?

1. They meet people for the first time, look them right in the eye, and make them feel comfortable.

2. They ask a question then listen intently and let you know they are talking to you.

3. They stay in contact and are very loyal to their friends.

4. If something crosses their desk that might be of interest, they will send it on.

5. They use humor and are equally at ease with both men and women.

6. They embrace people, not just the *right* people.

7. They make the connection, even if they just share a glance.

8. They exude confidence, yet appeal to the most average person.

But how do we become a person with whom people want to talk, to work, to collaborate, or to spend personal or professional time and energy? We must become savvy people who are aware of the unwritten rules for this process called networking. One must understand the politics of markers and owing chits.

Networking is an enrichment program, not an entitlement program. Too many people feel that under the guise of networking they are to be given leads, referrals, and information that they have not earned. We earn these leads by establishing communication and rapport.

We must reciprocate. Treat people with respect, courtesy, integrity, truth, and honor. People will do business with people they know, like, and trust.

People enjoy giving leads to others who have a track record and with whom there is a connection! We establish these connections by meeting and mingling and communicating.

Make It Easy to Work With You

1. Just say "no" to no-win networking. Our networks are too precious to include people who aren't appropriate, courteous, or competent.

2. Stay in touch with people when you need nothing from them.

3. Have fun and be of good humor, but *never* at the expense of others.

4. Pay attention and incorporate the rules—written and unwritten.

If we understand that savvy networkers are soft-sell and establish relationships in networks, we will be shining stars of the business community and in our personal endeavors. Savvy networkers share a skill with successful leaders: They are aware of their impact on others and behave accordingly. And they are aware of the favorbank: its deposits, withdrawals, and accrued interest.

Rather than view networking as a time waster, savvy networkers see it as an investment that may pay off for a designated receiver. Someone who was immense help to me in the early stages of my business asked me if I could help her daughter who had graduated from law school. It was my great pleasure to return my friend's assistance and support by helping her daughter. And, it relieved her of having to appear as a nagging parent.

By the same token, we get to call in favors to help our friends, colleagues, relatives, and cronies. Networking has been the way of the world. We just gave it a new term. It used to be called…helping!

Susan RoAne is a San Francisco based keynote speaker and bestselling author. Her printed books and audio books include *How to Work a Room* (revised edition) and her other bestselling books which include *The Secrets of Savvy Networking* and *What Do I Say Next*. All of her books are available through your local bookstores or from her website. Contact Susan at 415-239-2224 or view her books on www.SusanRoAne.com.

Don't Leave Home Without Your Business Cards
Renee Walkup

Since I am from a long line of entrepreneurs, I suppose it's in my blood to constantly think like a business owner. In that regard, it's my philosophy that I don't leave my house, office, or car without thinking that the next person I meet might be a potential business opportunity.

With that, I always—and I mean, always—have business cards with me because you just never know. I recommend that *you* always have cards with *you*—keep them in your wallet, your briefcase, your golf bag, your purse, your gym bag, your car, and even your diaper bag!

Yes, your diaper bag. Let me share a few examples of how being alert and having my cards with me has served my business well. Several years ago I had my infant daughter with me at the business club where I'm a member. On this day I was carrying only a diaper bag because I wasn't planning on conducting business. Ah, but I was! Because I always am. A gentleman approached our table to admire the baby, we struck up a conversation, and it turns out he was having breakfast with a high-powered executive of a company I had targeted to work with for a year.

He made the introduction and a successful business relationship ensued. The gentleman has since changed companies and we are still working together. You just never know where shameless self promotion might get you!

Just one more example of how you must always have your cards with you. I attended a neighborhood girl's night out get-together and met an executive with a major advertising company. Since I own a speaker's bureau and we are targeting ad agencies, my antennae was alerted when she mentioned her company. We chatted and I discovered that she was on the search committee to bring in trainers for her company's development. She didn't have her card with her, but this shameless self promoter *did*. I passed it on and she emailed me the next day.

I have dozens of these stories to share, but the main point is that you must always be prepared for the opportunity. I once heard of an extreme case of a shameless self promoter in the insurance business that put his business cards on the toilet seat of the restrooms during a funeral! That is going TOO far. However, what's to stop you from having your business cards and a pen just about everywhere you go?

So get to your printer and have another 1000 cards printed. You just never know where the next opportunity will knock!

> Renee P. Walkup is president and CEO of SalesPEAK, Inc. She provides speaking, training, and consulting services to those who want to achieve greater success in their professional lives. She can be reached at 770-220-0832 or view her website at www.salespeak.com.

Have I Told You What I've Done Lately?

Rochelle Balch

Do you really know what you do? Think about it. Let's say you're at a networking type event and everyone introduces themselves. You know the routine. You get 30 seconds to describe your life. Can you? So, what do you do?

A typical response may be something like this: I work at The Big Company in the shipping department and I've been there for over three years. The Big Company makes really big widgets and I make sure they get shipped out. The Big Company is best known for their Supreme Widgets, which they sell to regional widget suppliers.

Did you say what you do? Do you package the widgets? Do you check the packing slips? Do you count the boxes to be put on the truck? Do you pull the widgets from the shelves? Do you manage the group that does all of the above? Do you get the picture? In your head, in your mind, *you* know what you do, but someone else may not.

Why is this important? Because you never know when that opportunity may present itself for a great new job or position and you need to be ready. Basically, you need to know how to promote yourself. How to brag.

Remember when "to brag" had negative connotations? Well, get over it. Bragging is self promotion and we all need to know how to do it and how to feel comfortable about doing it.

Practice your 30-second commercial. Over and over and over again. This must flow off of your lips like water off the rocks of a waterfall. You have to be able to brag and not even need to think about it.

Let's try The Big Company scenario again: I'm with The Big Company in shipping. I verify that the right items are pulled and check to see that they are packed correctly. Over the last three years I've saved the company over $500,000 by catching incorrectly pulled items. I'm considered a senior quality control specialist.

Do you see the difference? You've stated what you do, you've stated that you made contributions to the company, and you've stated that you have a somewhat responsible position. And, you've said it in fewer words. It takes practice, but you can do it.

Self promotion is important if you own your own business, as you're always promoting your company. If you don't own your own company, self promotion is needed for advancement.

When considering "have I told you what I've done lately," remember to keep in mind who you need to tell, and who you need to impress.

High self-esteem promotes good self-confidence. Good self-confidence helps keep you motivated. You need to be motivated to brag. Self promotion is bragging. Then again, self promotion promotes self-confidence. Self-confidence promotes high self-esteem. Do you see how this all works together?

Why is self promotion—bragging—necessary? Put this all together and you reduce stress because you have a better ability to deal with stuff. Once you've been able to tell "them" what you do—promote yourself—you'll feel better about yourself.

Now, don't go overboard. Don't get obnoxious about it. Through trial and error, you'll discover the right amount of self promotion or self-gloating that is right for you.

> Rochelle Balch started a home-based computer consulting firm in 1993. As a result of shameless self promotion, Rochelle grew her business from $85,000 annual sales to well over $2 million today. Rochelle has received numerous business awards including Entrepreneur of the Year. Rochelle is the author of *CEO & MOM*, and her business has been featured on TV and radio and in magazines, including *Newsweek* and *Businessweek*. For more information, call her at 800-9-Balch-9 or view her website at www.RochelleBalch.com.

A Niche and a Network

Roseann Higgins

Meeting people is my livelihood since I'm a romance headhunter. I'm the only one in the country with this job title, since I created and federally trademarked the name of my business. The greatest difference between my business, **S.P.I.E.S.** (Single Professional Introductions for the Especially Selective), and other introduction services is that only one of the two people I bring together has to retain me.

The service is one-on-one and private. It attracts extremely eligible men and women. Some of the people I work with have appeared on CNN, CNBC, Larry King Live, and ESPN. And they've been written up in *Fortune Magazine, The Wall Street Journal, National Geographic,* and *Sports Illustrated.*

Finding a niche and creating a one-of-a-kind service to fill it, constantly telling people about my business, and seeking advice from PR experts and leading entrepreneurs has helped **S.P.I.E.S.** become the highest end, most talked about, most publicized introduction service in Arizona.

Choosing a memorable name was on my mind for weeks. When I thought of the name **S.P.I.E.S.**, I got excited! I asked 11 people I saw that day what they thought. The first two hated it. I could have stopped there and made a big mistake. But the next nine people thought **S.P.I.E.S.** was intriguing.

A marketing counselor at the Small Business Development Center invited me to present my concept to his MBA students at Western International University. I told them I was going to charge less than other dating services and offer more service. They advised, "You're offering more services, you should charge a premium. There will be a perceived value if you charge more. And you will get more publicity." I was skeptical, but they knew more about business than I did. When the next client asked how much, I monotoned, "Two thousand." I held my breath. They wrote the check. That was 1994; my fee is a little higher today. And **S.P.I.E.S.** has received over $50,000 worth of free publicity. The MBA students were right.

I've attended dozens of marketing and sales seminars looking for new ideas. Often keynote speakers live elsewhere and don't know anyone in town. Many of them don't rent cars because the hotel provides airport pickup and the host delivers them to the venue. When Jay Conrad Levinson, author of the *Guerrilla Marketing*™ series, was giving one of his signature high-speed, material-laden seminars to the Phoenix area chambers of commerce, I stuck around and asked for him to autograph one of his books. When I learned he was going to the airport, I asked if I could give him a ride.

On our way to the airport I told Jay that if he pushed up on the ceiling of my '84 Toyota Celica we could hear each other over the loud knocking noise from a bad cylinder when we hit 55 on the freeway. That was his first trip with me. He marveled at the like new '89 Mercedes 560 SL convertible with personalized **S.P.I.E.S.** license plates that I had when I gave him a lift a year later.

Thanks to Jay Conrad Levinson and other highly successful marketing experts whom I now count as my friends, I've received expensive business advice from the best for the price of taxi service to the airport or lunch. But before you insist on your own personal audience, it probably helped that I've invested thousands of dollars in these seminars, tapes, and books.

I've attended over 3,000 events and introduced myself to at least 30,000 people. I'm constantly grabbing newspapers and magazines at coffee shops and strategizing how to fit the best events onto my busy calendar. Meeting people is more costly and time consuming than mass marketing. Politicians are the only ones who go to more events than I do. No matter how much money they spend on signage, mailings, and TV spots, pressing the flesh is what wins elections.

Outsiders think I've pursued PR. No one in the local dating service industry gets as much coverage. I've traced 35 of 120 television, radio, newspaper, and magazine interviews to sitting at the right table at power breakfasts, association luncheons, and awards dinners with a reporter or someone who told a reporter about **S.P.I.E.S.**

What I've Learned About Self Promotion

I used to have a one-sided, two-color business card. Until I got some great advice, "The class of your service doesn't translate to your business card." My business card is now a showpiece. It's two-sided, folded over, embossed, gold foiled, with my color photo on the front and testimonials on the back. It's a mini-brochure on the inside. Now, when I give my business card to someone, other people want to know what I do and want a card, too.

Auctions at charity events are PR gold mines. At Alice Cooper's annual Solid Rock Foundation golf tournament, I won dinner for six with he and his wife Sheryl for $3,600. Then, I made out the guest list of people I knew and would like to know better. The first two people said yes, a national television morning show host and a Fortune 500 CEO. A society reporter from the major local daily newspaper learned of the dinner and featured it in her column. **S.P.I.E.S.** got great publicity and we all got to learn about when Alice Cooper met Elvis Presley.

Networking has presented opportunities to write for several publications. I wrote articles on networking for a business magazine in exchange for my photo and a full paragraph business byline. The articles were well worth the writing experience, the contacts, and the publicity. I received networking tips from Walter Cronkite and *Swim with the Sharks* author Harvey Mackay. It is a high profile way to advertise without selling and has resulted in new clients.

If you develop a niche or a specialty, meet new people like crazy, and are the best at what you do, people will write about you, talk about you, and do business with you.

> "If men are from Mars and women are from Venus, you'll probably find Roseann Higgins roaming both planets trying to match up her clients" FOX 10 Evening News. Roseann is the president of **S.P.I.E.S.** : Single Professional Introductions for the Especially Selective. She is a freelance writer for *Phoenix Magazine* and is writing her first book. Contact her directly at 602-241-1800 or by email at RoseannH@home.

If the Hat Fits, Wear It

Sandra Schrift

For the past four years, I have been attending networking events, meetings, conferences wearing one of my baseball style hats, my special style of branding. I now own four of these hats, to match my outfits. All the hats have the following inscription: "Speakers Business Coach."

These hats are great attention getters and conversation starters. When I wear a baseball hat, I bring attention to what I do. It also adds a dimension of lightness and fun. I want to attract clients who are the same.

The hat is a great way for clients to pick me out. Since I do most of my coaching by telephone, I sometimes meet a client for the first time at a conference. I tell them to look for my hat.

If I don't wear my hat to an event, people ask, "Where is your hat?" Or they say, "I didn't recognize you without your hat." I usually tell them that I wear the hat to cover up my bald spots!

A photo of me wearing a coach's hat is on my business card, every page of my website, and my brochure.

> Sandra Schrift is a career coach to emerging and experienced speakers on the business of speaking. She hosts Speaker University Tele-classes, an on-going series of classes for aspiring speakers, authors, coaches, entrepreneurs who want to go from free to a fee! Contact her and view her website at www.Schrift.com.

Self Promotion from the Personal Side

Craig Campana

My wife Linda and I used a form of self promotion we call networking when we decided to embark on a campaign to market ourselves as a childless couple seeking to adopt. We decided to "market" our needs to the contacts we knew. We decided to create a strong message and send it out to as wide an audience as possible. Although we didn't recognize it at the time, we were networking.

We created a business card with a simple message: "We desire to adopt." The card had a caricature of a duck and the phone number of an adoption hotline we had installed in our home. We had our photographs taken, and even produced a video showing my wife and me in family settings. (This seemed to be a novel idea in adoption circles.)

We added our adoption cards to an extended Christmas card list of 250 diverse contacts, including relatives, friends, high school and college contacts, church friends, co-workers, former co-workers, medical professionals, and members of the clergy. We gave our cards to anyone and everyone we met and asked each one to pass them along to anyone considering placing their baby for adoption. We also asked them to present, along with our cards, an endorsement for us as a couple. We believed that someone out there might know someone who could contact the right person.

Exactly one month after Christmas we received a call from one of those contacts who knew of a woman making an adoption plan for her unborn baby. To make a long story shorter, this woman decided she wanted us to become adoptive parents for her unborn child. Our son Corey was born in June 1991, and as we flew to Montana to receive him, we reflected on how, using a simple but creative means to self promote, we were able to achieve our goal. After many hours of planning, patience, persistence, marketing ourselves in some creative ways stood out in very productive ways. Ironically the one card we debated sending at all was the one that made the difference. The baby we adopted came from the person who received that card.

One aspect of self promotion that falls within the realm of networking is to understand what the top five networking traits are and how they apply to your business. I participated in a survey of more than 2,000 business people in the United States, Canada, United Kingdom, and Australia. The survey asked participants to rank a variety of traits in order of perceived importance to networking. The survey results were about the same for all four countries, which tells us that the principles of good networking transcend national and cultural boundaries. Those five traits are:

1. **Follows up on referrals:** This was ranked as the top trait of successful networkers. It's no secret that if you present opportunities, whether a simple piece of information, a special contact, or a qualified business referral, to someone who consistently fails to follow up successfully, you'll eventually stop wasting your time with this person.

2. **Positive attitude:** A consistently negative attitude makes people dislike you and drives away referrals; a positive attitude makes people want to associate and cooperate with you.

3. **Enthusiasm/Motivation:** Think about the people you know. Who gets the most referrals? People who show the most motivation, right? It has been said that the best sales characteristic is enthusiasm. To be respected within our networks, we at least need to sell ourselves.

4. **Trustworthiness:** When you refer one person to another, you put your reputation on the line. You have to be able to trust your referral partner and be trusted in return. Neither you nor anyone else will refer a contact or valuable information to someone who can't be trusted to handle it well.

5. **Good listening skills:** Our success as networkers depends on how well we can listen and learn. The faster you and your networking partner learn what you need to know about each other, the faster you'll establish a valuable relationship. Communicate well, and listen well.

Used with permission from *Masters of Networking*, by Dr. Ivan R. Misner and Don Morgan, Bard Press, Austin, Texas.

> Craig Campana is an author, speaker, and networking trainer. He founded the first chapter of Business Network International in Wisconsin. Craig is a contributing author to the book *Masters of Networking*, which has been on the *Wall Street Journal* and *New York Time*'s best-seller list. He is currently authoring a new book titled *Turning Career Adversity Into Power For Success*. Contact Craig at 262-781-7194 or view his website at www.bniwis.com.

Chapter Eight

Building Your Unique Brand Recognition

*If you truly expect to realize your dreams,
abandon the need for blanket approval.
If conforming to everyone else's expectations
is the number one goal, you have sacrificed your
uniqueness and, therefore, your excellence.*

—Don Ward

Shameless Self Promotion Step 8: Break the Mold, Then Shamelessly Promote Your Uniqueness

Debbie Allen

Remember My Name

In today's business world of growing competition both on and off the Web, it is crucial to create a unique identity or brand for yourself and your business—no matter how small or how large your business may be.

Debbie Allen is a famous actress and choreographer who introduced the musical and TV show *Fame* to the world.

People often joke with me. "Are you really the famous Debbie Allen?" To that I reply, "Of course I am—I'm the Debbie Allen of marketing fame." This is an easy way for me to get people to remember my name. The theme to *Fame* includes the words, "Remember, remember my name." These words sing the message of the first part of my uniqueness: People *do* remember my name.

I use this opportunity to tell people more about my business. I used to say, "I'm a professional speaker." But most people would get a puzzled look on their faces, then say, "Oh, you're a motivational speaker, like Anthony Robbins." I realized that most people have no idea what a professional speaker does. I found myself explaining that although I hoped that most people would find my presentations motivational, I did not require anyone to walk over hot coals.

I finally realized that I was missing the chance to give an effective commercial about my business. Now I share my branded catch praise: "I help businesses to Out-Market, Out-Sell, and Out-Profit their competition. I do this through professional speaking, consulting, personal coaching, and writing." This explains it much better, and it turns the confused looks and raised eyebrows to understanding. Their interest is piqued and they want to know more what I offer my clients. This leaves the door open for self promotion and interesting conversations.

Another effective way I have branded myself is to become the creator and founder of special events. Not only is this a great way to get media exposure, it builds the basis for my specialization. For example, I am the founder of "Self Promotion Month/October" and "International Business Image Improvement Month/May." Sounds impressive, doesn't it?

Anyone can be an expert on something and then turn their expertise into a special event for the world to celebrate. Here's how:

Think about your expertise and then brainstorm to come up with your own special event. Next, write a short paragraph describing your event and offer a free service or valuable information for free. Then send it in to *Chase's Calendar of Events* and *Celebrate Today*. If your special event is accepted (and most are), they post your listing at no charge. The media constantly uses these resources to write articles and search for radio and television guest experts. You could be the expert and the next story they are looking for. Contact information for these publications are listed on page 231.

Here is a list of my special events, or see Gail Howerton's confessions (page 139) for another example.

Self Promotion Month (October 1-31)

Learn how to toot your own horn and promote your business to another level of success. Unique marketing strategies with a twist are shared by some of the most successful marketing gurus in the nation. Discover some of these insightful and shameless marketing strategies. Receive your free subscription to *Confessions of Shameless Self Promoters* online newsletter at www.ConfessionsofShamelessSelfPromoters.com. This electronic newsletter is published by international professional speaker, author and marketing consultant, Debbie Allen. Contact Debbie Allen at (800) 359-4544 for more information on this special event.

International Business Improvement Month (May 1-31)

The image of your business sets the tone for how successful your company will be. Just as we judge others within the first few seconds of meeting, we do the same for a business. Receive more information on how to improve your business image and a free business card evaluation. For information contact Debbie Allen at 800-359-4544, fax 480- 831-8334, or email at Debbie@DebbieAllen.com.

Capitalize on Your Uniqueness

Larry Winget

"Discover your uniqueness and learn to exploit it in the service of others and you are guaranteed success, happiness, and prosperity."

That is the smartest thing I ever said. It is the essence of my success and the essence of what this book on self promotion is about. No individuals or businesses can effectively market themselves until they know who they are and have discovered their uniqueness.

Fortunately, we all have uniqueness. Unfortunately, few of us ever discover it. The key is to first identify what is *not* your uniqueness; we all know what that is. Your uniqueness is probably *not* the thing you are doing for a living and *not* the thing that you are using to market yourself. And then we wonder why we are unhappy and are not experiencing any success.

I know who I am. I know what makes me unique, and I have spent my career capitalizing on it. I have a unique appearance. Not that others don't look like me, but I was the first in my business with the shaved head, goatee, and earring. For many years, I coupled that with very interesting glasses. (At this point I have over 60 pairs of glasses.) And while I no longer wear the red, black and white checks, purple and green paisley, or lime green pairs, I still wear very interesting glasses. And I wear black, almost exclusively. I might throw on a bright red, yellow, blue, or purple sportcoat, but I still primarily wear black. This may not sound that unique but, again, I work in a business that is mostly suits, white shirts, and ties. I never wear a tie, and I stand out.

My style and delivery are unique as well. I have taken a different angle than my colleagues. Instead of being known as a motivational speaker, I bill myself as "The World's Only Irritational Speaker™!" I am also known as the "Pitbull of Personal Development™!" I do "Hardcore Self-Help that's Funny™!" I have given myself these labels and trademarked them in order to very clearly identify who I am and what I do. I stomp on your toes and make you laugh.

Caution! The key to all of this is to not get *too* weird. Weird is a liability. People do not really want weird, at least not in big doses. And they certainly won't pay well for it. Who does better at the movies, Tom Cruise or Weird Al Yankovic? And don't make the mistake of thinking that unique means different. People don't really want different either. But they will pay a premium for unique. It applies to fashion, furniture, houses, real estate, and people.

I am known for certain sayings and ideas. I became so identified with certain words that, those in the speaking industry have said that I actually own those words. One of those words is "stuff." Most of my book titles include that word, and I exploit it on my website as well.

I also am known for the philosophy, "Shut Up, Stop Whining, and Get a Life™!" I have it on shirts, hats, mugs, mousepads, pens, buttons, and about anything else I can print it on. The same goes for "If Your Life Sucks, It's Because You Suck!" As a result of the popularity of that line, I created an entire line of products called "USUK™." That is an example of my style being unique. It sets me apart from other speakers because it is so contrary to what is typically said onstage. This is also a message that is a bit over the edge and creates an emotional response. When you combine the message and the emotion it makes *me*, the guy who delivers it, memorable. That is what we should all be going for: being memorable.

When the WWF and other pro wrestling syndicates became so amazingly popular, I took advantage of their New World Order (NWO) and created Larry World Order (LWO). I printed shirts with my own beliefs on them and distributed them. Some didn't get it (sometimes you are just too hip for the room) and some loved them. The point here is that I capitalized on a trend, personalized without plagiarizing, then exploited it within my market. We all see it all the time. Look at any trend and then watch how the whole market becomes flooded with things that are similar yet different enough to be unique.

We see this in television all the time. *Who Wants to be a Millionaire* becomes a hit, then *Greed* and other similar shows follow. The key is to either be first or to do it better or faster or funnier or *something*. You want to capitalize on the trend without blatantly ripping it off. You never want to lose your market's respect. Instead you want them to applaud your guts, your creativity, your uniqueness, and your sense of humor.

Results: What I do works. I keep hammering in who I am and what I do over and over and over and over again until I am sure that when someone hears the name Larry Winget they will know exactly what I do. And when anyone needs services such as mine, my name will automatically come to mind.

Discover your uniqueness and learn to exploit it. In my business that means exploitation in print, audio, video, CD, and any other way that you can think of. I have branded my name and I have done it by making my image memorable and my message (my product) so tied to me that if anyone dares to steal it, they will be looked at as a wannabe Larry. This can be done by anyone with any product. Just discover your uniqueness and exploit it!

Try everything and listen to no one. Try everything that sounds like a good idea to you. I don't want anyone else's opinion. I don't trust *anyone* to know how to market me but me. And I try everything. I try it first on a small scale and if I get any positive response, then I expand it until it touches everyone I market to. You have to play the numbers and you have to take risks. Some people won't like what I do, and that is fine. I don't need or want their business. I want to do business with the people who are in sync with me.

> Larry Winget is a philosopher of success. As a professional speaker and author of numerous books, Larry teaches universal principles that will work for anyone, in any business, at any time. He does this by telling funny stories. Larry can be reached at 800-749-4597 or view his website at www.LarryWinget.com.

The BITCH with Style

Dr. Vikki Ashley

Let me establish right up front that some of the "products" that I am marketing to the world are in my first two books: *How to Be a BITCH with Style: Being in Total Control of Herself (B.I.T.C.H.)* and *Alan's Song of Love: Our AIDS Odyssey.* My "products" are ideas, processes, and experiences, all of which come from my most important product, *me.* I express some of my products in my books, as well as my seminars and healing activities (hypnosis, past-life regressions, relaxation therapy, energy medicine, and creative visualization.) But it is me, *c'est moi*, that I am really marketing and promoting.

Every single thing I do is energy/spirit based, soul focused, and health oriented. I must be proud of my ideas, processes, and experiences and own each and every one. If I can't or won't, why should anyone else? If you have courage, you will cultivate this shameless self promoter approach to living. Why? Because you will be able to accept full and total responsibility for every aspect of your life. You will put on your oxygen mask before you presume to help anyone else breathe!

Your cup will be half-full, not half-empty, and you will harbor no anger, resentment, or hostility toward anyone else in the world. You will be in total control of yourself and your life!

Becoming a shameless self promoter requires some very fundamental steps and some deep thought. It doesn't just happen. Here they are:

Seven Steps to Your Unique Marketing Principle (UMP)

Step 1: Attention
Red is my signature color. Everywhere I go I wear a gorgeous red hat and red outfits to stand out from the crowd. Am I noticed? You bet! Do I get attention? You bet! Do people remember me? You bet! If no one notices you and your ideas, processes, and experiences, there's no way to promote whatever vehicle you used to express them.

Step 2: Branding

There aren't too many books out there that look like mine. The logo, colors, and name were designed around the acronym BITCH (Being In Total Control of Herself). I've created a complete series of collateral products associated with the book. These products include tee shirts (with twelve steps to BITCHhood on the back), mugs, notepads, a refrigerator magnet, and the BITCH's Book Bag, which I carry with me on trips. These items are for sale, but their greatest benefit has been for marketing and promotion. BITCH is everywhere.

Step 3: Communication

Traveling the two-way street of communication is what selling ideas is all about. The Unique Marketing Principle (UMP) is your *interactive logo and design* that fairly makes you want to communicate with whomever is wearing or carrying an item with your logo or unique slogan one it. Again, it sets up a buzz and starts everyone talking about that BITCH! No, that BITCH *with style.*

Step 3: Distinctive

Be yourself no matter what *other people* say. A creative and distinctive approach, product, or idea is worth millions. Take the time to think through your approach. Keep in mind that *your thoughts control your life.* Don't run with the herd. Instead, lift your sights and soar. Dare to be distinctive.

Step 4: Energy

Whatever you do, think of energy. Energy is spirit/vibration. When I thought about what I wanted to do with my book and products, I thought about the following facets of energy: thoughts, words, color, sound, physical image, and, above all, psychological strength and courage to do whatever it takes to implement the plan.

Step 5: Head Turner

This is the wow factor of whatever you do. When you walk past something and go back to take a look and say, "*wow!*" Or you point to something different and distinctive and say "Wow! What a great idea!" Or "Wow! Look at her!" or "Wow, I wish I'd done that!" This is an exponential leap beyond just getting attention. Knock 'em out with your uniqueness and willingness to be different. Turn heads!

Step 6: Innovate

Innovation is a powerful concept. It means to introduce something new or to introduce change. Individuals resist change. However, until they *do* change spiritually, mentally, emotionally and physically, they can't grow. Neither can ideas. Marketing and promotion are in the province of change and getting someone out there to buy whatever it is you're selling. Breaking down the customer's resistance to your ideas, processes, and experiences is a large part of business success. In fact, it is *the most important aspect* of marketing and promotion.

Innovation forces you to think for yourself and to stop value judging. Then it provides the impetus to brainstorm and mind map diverse ways of thinking, new windows of perception, discover hidden talents, new ways of saying old things, new networks and contacts, and ways to integrate all aspects of your life, Most importantly, it reinvents not only your ideas, processes, and experiences, but you.

Step 7: JUST DO IT!

> Dr. Vikki Ashley describes herself as a dynamic "Cosmic Spark Plug." She is an author, communicator, transformational psychologist, clinical hypnotherapist, musician, executive coach and mentor, management consultant, and, best of all, shameless self promoter. Contact Dr. Vikki at 504-895-7968 or view her website at www.bitchwithstyle.com.

Discovering Your Core Essence

Gail Howerton

As a professional speaker, trainer, author, and facilitator of fun and effectiveness, my first and foremost job is to be a shameless self promoter and unabashed marketing maven. Even if we have the greatest, latest product on the market, if nobody knows about it, then we do everybody a disservice. The public goes without our product, message, or service and we go without customers, food on the table, or a self-sustaining business. Everybody loses.

Once I changed my perception from "selling myself and my services as the product" to "serving others in helping them get what they want to improve the quality of their lives," my whole trepidation about polite girls not blowing their own horns also changed dramatically. It became much easier to focus on the benefits-based marketing because I knew the information I could share would dramatically improve people's lives. I could help them organize and energize; have more fun at work; balance their personal and professional lives; practice safe stress; enhance their performance; save time, effort, and money; and improve their personal energy. It became very exciting to figure out creative ways to let others know about how I could help them lead better lives.

Knowing your purpose, vision, mission, and uniqueness is the foundation on which all marketing is built. Discovering your core essence—who you are, what you want, and how you want to live and serve—is ground zero for building your image, your brand, and your position in the marketplace. Become keenly aware of where your curiosity, interests, and intuition lead you.

"Do what you love and the money will follow" is my mantra. Even though many people questioned a business of providing fun to the workplace ("Can you get paid for that? Are you sure you want to leave your government job?"), I was sure I wanted to work for more than a good dental plan. I felt this was my calling. After all, my parents always said I love to have fun and I talk a lot. I was perfect for this job! I even had an authentic credential: Certified Leisure Professional.

Once I knew my special traits included boundless energy, deft organizational skills, and an unsinkable sense of adventure, and fun, I combined those with my background in recreation and experiential education. With a decade of living and working overseas facilitating international leisure and learning, I came up with the company name, Fun*cilitators. The name says that we facilitate fun and effectiveness and cover many aspects of the business: speaking, training, teambuilding, consulting, facilitating, and writing. I also chose a moniker other than my own name since my name may change in the future and I wanted to build a brand around Fun*cilitators.

Once I had developed the company name and tag lines, I set to work on the rest of the corporate image. I wanted one that matched my personality—casual, fun, playful, energetic, and a little bit off-center. I started with the corporate colors, purple and teal. I chose purple because it is the most vibrant, creative color of the spectrum and is rich and powerful with a playful edge. (Think Barney.) I sign all the business correspondence in purple and have a lot of purple in my wardrobe. I opted for a casual, hand-drawn feel to the font style and company logo to create an image that is playful, fun, casual, and a bit cartoonish.

From this base there flowed an unending stream of ideas to carry on this message. They allowed me to position myself, claim a niche, and develop a brand identity. It is all about consistent repetitions so people remember you. If your image is in alignment with who you are, it just comes naturally.

Shameless Promotional Ideas that Have Worked for Me

▼ *Plastic Any Key* that sticks onto a computer keyboard and includes my contact information. This faux computer key has the words *any key* printed on the top. It attaches to a computer keyboard. This ties into my seminar topic, "Hit any key to energize your life." I give these away at trade shows, or stick them in correspondence envelopes. I have found that if people feel that there is a prize inside the envelope, they're more likely to open it.

▼ *Fun Meter* button, with a pointer that moves from minimum to maximum. The meter includes my logo, toll-free number, and website. This is a wearable button that displays how much fun the wearer is having. It is adjusted by manually moving the meter from minimum to maximum.

▼ *National events sponsored by Fun*cilitators* which help others celebrate my message. I have submitted the following two events to the following resource books that list special event days, weeks, and months: *Chase's Calendar of Events* and *Celebrate Today*, which are mentioned at the beginning of this chapter. For example, I created National Promote Playful Professionalism Week and National Energize Your Life Week.

▼ *Postage stamp sized stickers* that feature the cover of my book and my website. I put one on every envelope that leaves my office.

▼ *My website* is the most critical piece of my marketing mix. The site features over 150 resources, a list of clients, testimonials, audio clips from radio talk shows, a demo video clip, a free monthly online newsletter, free articles, and background information on my services and myself.

As Zig Ziglar says, "If you help enough people get what they want, then you'll get what you want." There are plenty of people out there who are overworked, overwhelmed, overstressed, and overdue for a personal overhaul. What keeps me promoting unabashedly is the adventure of discovering new ways to bring benefits and value to their lives, while adding value and quality to my own.

Gail Howerton, MA, CLP (Certified Leisure Professional—an authentic credential), is the CEO (Chief Energizing Officer) at Fun*cilitators, which promotes peak performance through playful professionalism by facilitating fun and effectiveness through keynotes and workshops. She is the author of *Hit Any Key to Energize Your Life.* Contact Gail at 800-930-6096 or view her website at www.Funcilitators.com.

Seven Step Action Plan to Create a Marketing Brand
Burt Dubin

As a successful, journeyman-level speaker back in the late 1980s, I routinely received total fees each year well into six figures for 50 to 80 three-hour programs. As an active member of National Speakers Association, I watched the revolving door of wanna-be's come and go every month. I was dismayed to see that a full third of the NSA membership changed every year. As a skilled researcher I'd cracked the code. The secrets of getting a gig or two every week were no secret to me. I was doing it.

Action and Outcomes

I said to myself, "I can change this tragic loss of talent. I can show speakers how to do what I do." As a marketer, I knew I had to stand out from all others. I had to be unique and "unduplicatable"—to create a marketing brand unique to me.

Here is how to do what I do:

Action 1. Market the Outcome of Your Services, Not the Services Themselves.
I market success in the business of speaking. Eleven years after I first launched this concept, there is still nobody else has who has the audacity to copy what I am doing.

Action 2. Give a Money-Back Guarantee—in Writing, with Teeth.
During the first few years, I gave back some money. Since 1995 nobody has legitimately requested their money back.

Action 3. Don't Allow Scoundrels to Get at You.
Make your guarantee conditional upon specific performance by the other person. Mine is simple. "Do what I guide you to do and document to me that you have done so." That's all you need to protect yourself from scoundrels.

Action 4. Do Exhaustive Research.

Spare no expense. Make yourself the very best on earth at what you do. Do more than is required. Do more than is expected. Do more that anyone in their right mind would do. Be the very best at what you do.

Action 5. Stimulate Referrals.

Reward your clients or customers who refer you to folks who invest in what you offer. Give appropriate gifts, depending on the size of the ticket and reward referrals generously.

Action 6. Treat People Right.

Be there for them long after the sale. Care about each client. You've heard this before: "People don't care about how much you know until they know how much you care!" Let the Golden Rule govern your attitudes, your thoughts, your words, and your actions.

Action 7. Don't Sell—Market.

What's the difference? Selling is persuading someone to buy your wares. Marketing is creating conditions under which the buyer is attracted to your offer and decides on their own to invest in what you offer. How do you do that? Public relations. Advertising. Word-of-mouth.

In the words of Walt Disney, "Do what you do so well that people can't resist coming back for more and telling their friends to do the same."

> Burt Dubin is president of Personal Achievement Institute. Burt is publisher of the Speaking Success System. To view free downloadable articles and for your free subscription to the *Speaking Biz Success Letter* search his website at www.SpeakingSuccess.com. You may reach Burt directly at 520-753-7546.

A Spy Is Born

Anne M. Obarski

As a retail speaker and trainer in the early 1980s, I did countless programs on buying, selling, and merchandising techniques to all sizes of retailers nationwide. My audiences would nod their heads in approval, take copious notes, and go back to their stores all fired up. Within days they were back to their same old habits. Sounds like church!

In 1985, a retail friend of mine suggested that I try to develop a "secret shopper" program. I had worked in retail for many years and knew what that term meant. To most managers the words meant "panic." Why? Because at some time, a spy would wander into their store, unannounced, and critique everything and everyone, then leave like a thief in the night. The spy would send a report to management with the ratings and comments about their shopping experience. Management's reaction would vary from pure anger to shear delight. (Rarely was it the later.)

So why would I even consider adding a new area to my business that would make people angry with me? The answer is simple. It was a guaranteed way to help stores accurately measure what their customers see, hear and feel when they deal with that store. This research would pinpoint the areas in which they excel and those in which they need to improve. And all of this research comes directly from the client's most important asset, their customer. A secret shopper program would make my training completely customized to that client. They'd have a "report card" with specific areas to address.

So in 1985, the Retail Snoops part of my business was born. I put on a trench coat and a dark wig and, with a simple questionnaire in hand, began "shopping" for excellence in customer service. Over the past 15 years, my company has shopped over 5,000 stores looking for that excellence. Guess what? We are still looking.

While I developed questionnaires for other companies, I found myself focusing on my own business. Here are some questions I asked myself:
- ▼ How professional does my advertising look?
- ▼ Is my marketing unique and does it focus on my branded image?
- ▼ How do I answer the phone?

▼ Do I return phone calls promptly?
▼ Do I have value based pricing?
▼ Do I treat my customers like royalty?
▼ Do my customers provide me with repeat and referral business?

All this examination made me go back to my mission statement and unique branding to see if I was really providing what I advertised!

I promote myself as the "eye on retail performance"! My "eyes" now not only see what areas my clients want me to focus on, but they look inward to see if I am offering excellence in my business performance.

How do you see yourself? Are you ready and willing to take a closer look at your uniqueness?

Anne Obarski is the owner of Merchandise Concepts, a retail consulting service. Speaker, trainer, and author of the workbook *Applied Retail Mathematics,* Anne works with organizations who want to retain their employees and their customers. Her Retail Snoops secret shopper program helps companies discover the clues to improving their businesses. To contact Anne call 800-506-1144, ext 4551 or view her website at www.MerchandiseConcepts.com.

Finding Your Specialization

Gwen Ashley Walters

Marketing is as old as trade itself, and as natural as breathing. Some people are born with the innate ability to sell, while others develop it as a skill. I fall into the latter category. I'm still developing and honing my skill. It's a life-long work-in-progress.

Selling, marketing, and promotion are three separate functions but all interconnected. Promotion is a function of marketing, and marketing is a function of selling. I tend to use the three terms interchangeably, but the bottom line is about selling a product, whatever that product might be.

In my case, I am the product. I sell me. Who better to sell me, than me? I have "line-extensions," such as my books and teaching, but I am the brand, not my books or my classes. I use these ancillary products as tools to promote my product—me. I am the authority on travel-destination cooking. That statement is my mission.

I haven't reached the pinnacle of my mission yet, but that's not the point. The point is, I have a mission statement, and everything I do is in sync with that. For each new opportunity presented to me I ask, "Does it fit my mission?" If not, I pass on it. There are very few "generalist" success stories in my culinary field. Even the top players are specialists: Julia Child and French cooking, Wolfgang Puck and catering to the stars, and Alice Waters and organic farming, for example.

It is that *specialization* that is the first of the major marketing hurdles you need to clear before you can be successful.

Three years ago, when I decided that I would write a cookbook, there were more than 8,000 cookbook titles available. That is an enormous amount of clutter to break through. I'd just come off of a summer of managing a guest ranch in southern Montana, and my husband suggested I write a guest ranch cookbook. Traveling around the West, eating glorious food and checking out resorts masquerading as dude ranches sounded like a fun job. Hey, somebody had to do it.

My vision was of a combination travel guide and cookbook, featuring high-end guest ranches that employed professional chefs. There wasn't anything like it on the market. I had passed the first marketing hurdle, establishing a point of differentiation.

I constantly think about how to tell more people about my books and me. Every encounter I have is churned in my mind for an angle. "How can I make this work for me?" Shameless? Sure, but if I don't sell me, who will?

> Gwen Ashley Walters, CCP is a professionally trained chef and Certified Culinary Professional. In addition to authoring travel-destination cookbooks, Gwen is a cooking teacher and food writer. She is the author of *The Great Ranch Cookbook: Spirited Recipes and Rhetoric from America's Best Guest Ranches* and *The Cool Mountain Cookbook: A Gourmet Guide to Winter Retreats.* Gwen may be reached at 480-488-2202 or view her website at www.PenandFork.com.

A "Brand" New You with a Big Brand Bank Account!

Anne Marie Baugh

The good ol' American cowboy still lays an iron in the fire and brands his beef with the proud mark of ownership. Branding in the business world is not so very different. It is the means for marking in the public mind a strong identity—an identity that is you and your company, forever.

If you're smart, you will make doubly sure that the process of branding you is marked with a strong sense of pride and personality that you back up with your personal integrity. After all, branding is something the public will remember forever, so you want them to remember you in the best and brightest possible light, right?

I recently had a client ask me why his press kit had to have so much information about him, the person, instead of just his business. As his publicist I took the time to explain that when the media comes to interview him it's not his business that will create the story, it's him! The person behind the business is the humanizing ingredient that will capture the attention of the public and create a sense of bonding that will in turn bring about more business. You are the key! Only people can create confidence and trust. And while products are branded everyday, branding you will create a deeper and more lasting impression.

Do you know anyone that ever tried to follow in the footsteps of say, Coca Cola? Of course not! But many an entrepreneur has tried to emulate the business icon Lee Iacocca. Now here is a man who understood the value of branding himself. Even at the helm of Chrysler he knew that to steer the failing automotive company into a position of profitability and drive the Chrysler mark into the minds of Americans again, he had to give it a voice. It had to be a voice that people could trust, a human voice. That voice was his. He was a man of leadership. His legend will forever be linked to the success of Chrysler.

So now the question is what will your brand say about you? What is the message you want to share with the world; that will become your mark, forever identifying your business and what it stands for? This is a bit akin to selecting your motto, the saying that forever tags along with your company name as a further identification of what you do. Your brand, however, says what you are! It is the characteristics and values that will become your public story.

Take time before you answer because forever is, well, forever! It is very important that you carefully consider what you want your story to be. To be effective and stand apart from the flood-gating crowd of the business world, it is especially important that the story of you, the story that will become your brand, rise above the rest in the madding crowd. So *please* resist copying or following. Be creative, be positively outrageous, be irresistible, but above all, be yourself in your approach.

Sound painful? Well, trust me, it's not. There's a wonderful new you with a wonderful new bank account coming your way. Simply put, branding you is the most important step to building more profits in your business. And profiting is never painful, is it?

> Anne Marie Baugh has worked in publicity and promotion for more than 20 years. She owns and operates five interlocking firms and has worked with a diverse selection of companies and individuals, from Fortune 1,000 firms, to start up companies. Contact her directly at anne@write-promotion.com or view her website at www.Write-Promotion.com.

> *I'm always me.*
> *You guys just take a while to catch up.*
>
> —Cher

Chapter Nine
Delivering Shamelessly Through the Mail

Small opportunities are often the beginning of great enterprises.

—Demosthenes (discovered more treasure from shipwrecks than anyone else in history)

Shameless Self Promotion Step 9:
Get Out in Front of Your Target Audience On a Regular Basis and Don't Ever Stop Reminding Them About Your Business

Debbie Allen

I confess: I love marketing! A constant reexamining approach and some smart business strategies have always gotten me through tough times. And that's what I love about marketing. I know that if I keep building my database and sending out direct mail, my business will grow. Of course, by adding other marketing strategies, it will grow even faster.

Marketing is like fishing. You discover where the fish are and you go there to start fishing. You get some bait, put it on your hook, throw out line after line, and change your bait every once in a while. Then you wait to catch fish. You know if you wait and fish long enough you are going to catch one or lots of them. The same is true for marketing. When you are doing it well you see results, though it might take some time to hook 'em.

During my 15 years as a retail business owner, I learned the importance of direct mail. This has always been one of the most effective forms of marketing for me. It is a simple approach that makes sense. If you send out six to eight direct mail pieces a year to each customer on your database, you are going to get more business than your competition who only does two to four mailings a year. So get the mail out to get business.

Ten Rules for Effective Direct Mail Design and Strong Visibility

1. Feature benefits.

2. Be creative and stand out from your competition.

3. Under promise and over deliver.

4. Use graphics and color to enhance your copy.

5. Do not print headlines or subheads in hard-to-read text.

6. Be consistent with your business image and logo recognition.

7. Make it easy for recipients to respond.

8. Carve your mail date in stone and plan well in advance.

9. Make an offer than can't be refused.

10. If sending a letter always add a P.S. If your readers don't read anything else, they are likely to read the P.S.

Resources for direct mail postcards, promotional mailers, and flyers are listed on page 231.

Bug 'Em 'Til They Buy or Die

George Hedley

I hate cold calls, but I love it when future customers call me. So I developed a marketing plan that doesn't require cold calls. It's more like that Chinese water torture you see in the old movies—drip, drip, drip. I call it: "Bug 'Em 'Til They Buy or Die!"

Three Steps to Get Them to Call You:

Awareness: Creates interest in *you*
Interest: Keeps *you* at the top of their mind
Top of Mind: Gets them to call *you* when they need you

Using my "Bug 'Em 'Til They Buy or Die" plan builds awareness of *you* and what you'll do for *them* over a period of time. (Drip.)

Awareness is based upon the Rule of Seven: You must have at least seven contacts with a future customer before they:

▼ Remember *your* name
▼ Feel they *know* and trust *you*
▼ Will call *you*

In my business I use the post office to make future customers aware of me. (Drip.) My office mails something to everyone on our mailing list at least six times per year. (Drip.) Once is not enough. (Drip, drip.) But we don't just send any old boring piece of mail. We send creative, different, unique, and informative "Bug 'Em 'Til They Buy or Die" mail. (Drip.) We use a professional design firm to keep our image consistent. (Drip.) Orange is my branded color. Everyone recognizes my orange hardhat on every piece of "Bug 'Em 'Til They Buy or Die" mail. (Drip, drip, drip.) I'm building awareness.

To create interest and be remembered, get different, crazy, and unique. Stand out from the crowd. Be clever, creative, and fun. Never send the same old throw-away pens, ball caps, and notepads that everyone else sends. Send professionally created materials that consistently reflect your message.

Quality counts. Match your "Bug 'Em 'Til They Buy or Die" mail to your future customer. I use a newsletter that looks like a blueprint for our construction customers, but to attract bank investors we use traditional white stationary with blue ink. Future customers respond to the familiar.

To peak the customer's interest we mail cartoons, jokes, small hardhats, estimating grid notepads, coffee cups with hammer handles, golf tees, golf ball markers, chads from election ballots (during the Bush/Gore election), and American flags on the Fourth of July! Once we mailed envelopes filled with nails and a banner that read "When can we nail down your next job?" Last year I sent postcards from Vail, Colorado with this note: "Thanks to my loyal customers for sending me skiing. I appreciate your business!"

Remember your goal is not only to create interest but to create the right kind of interest in you. You have to tell your future customers what you want them to *remember about you*. To show future customers that we were more than a local company, we sent out a map indicating our project locations within a 100-mile radius. To create a perception of fast service, we mailed out "on-time schedulers." Tell future customers what you want them to remember—over and over and over!

Getting future customers to call *you* is a long (drip), slow (drip) process (drip) that requires constant (drip) action (drip) over (drip) time. It will take one to two years to be effective. Marketing is a drip-drip-drip process. It is never a one-time event. I've sent "Bug 'Em 'Til They Buy or Die" mail every two months since 1984. I've never stopped because it works! I always get lots of future customer calls after every mailing. They call me!

And it's affordable! We typically mail "Bug 'Em 'Til They Buy or Die" mail to 1,000 to 2,000 future customers six times per year. The average cost (including postage) is $1.00 to $2.00 for each piece we mail. (Drip, drip.) Our annual "Bug 'Em 'Til They Buy or Die" budget for six mailings runs between $6,000 to $12,000. (Drip.) It's worth every penny—times ten!

We use a $200 database contact software program to keep track of future customers. The software sorts by address, industry, customer type, or any other criteria we need. You can also create personalized form letters to mail. It only takes a few minutes to print 1,000 mailing labels! Easy.

We dedicate four hours every month to our "Bug 'Em 'Til They Buy or Die" mailing program. We constantly look for great ideas, articles, perfect mailing pieces, and photo opportunities. To remain consistent, we've used the same professional design firm for over 20 years. But you can easily hire local marketing or graphic design students from nearby colleges to help you get started.

After we select and design our "Bug 'Em 'Til They Buy or Die" mail, the task of creating it in-house, using an outside promotional products vendor, or getting it to the printer is simple. When we are ready to mail, we use temporary help to print the labels, assemble the packages, and stuff the envelopes. Done.

I like the old saying: "Any plan is better than a perfect plan never executed." The key to "Bug 'Em 'Til They Buy or Die" mail is to do it! Every two months! Rain or Shine! So get started today and future customers will call you soon!

> George Hedley is the owner of a $100 million company and recipient of the nationally recognized "Entrepreneur of the Year" award. He also owns HARDHAT Presentations and speaks to companies on building leaders, loyal customers and profits. Contact George at 800-851-8553 or view his website at www.HardHatPresentations.com. To share your "Bug 'Em 'Til They Buy or Die" ideas with George, email him at gh@hardhatpresentation.com.

Leave Breadcrumbs

W Mitchell

The challenge is that most people don't care what we can do for them because they are focused on all the same stuff we are focused on, like stopping to pick up our dry cleaning or whether we need to put gas in the car. You must find a way that will interrupt their thinking and then leave "breadcrumbs" so that later they can come back to find you. Otherwise they are not going to remember you.

We shovel out a lot of business cards, marketing pieces, and brochures, but often they don't have a real grab factor that excites people! They don't give people something of value that they have reason to keep. Who is going to keep your business card? What do you do with business cards? Business cards are only good for transferring information temporarily. Other than that, most people simply throw them away. If you are going to use business cards to market yourself, at least add some helpful information to the back that people will want to keep in their wallets or on their desks.

Instead of a business card, I use a 3" x 4" postcard that states, "It's not what happens to you; it's what you do about it." The card includes a great graphic, my signature, and a small amount of contact information on the front. On the back it has more information about my business and additional quotes. I also use this message in a handsome Lucite cardholder with my card permanently enclosed. It is expensive but it stays around forever.

This billboard or message helps people take responsibility for change. I have discovered that some people keep these around for years because of the useful quote and nontraditional business card size.

I recently received a call from a man in London who has had one of my cards in his office for about ten years. He not only kept my card, but he also had the information on how to get a hold of me for all those years.

Leave "breadcrumbs" by sending something people will have an interest in retaining. It will pay off for you for years to come.

W Mitchell is a professional speaker and author of *It's Not What Happens to You, It's What You do About It*. His spellbinding message is about taking responsibility for change and how people can deal with setbacks and put themselves back in charge. Mitchell shows how to climb out of mental wheelchairs and break out of self-imposed prisons. Contact Mitchell at 800-421-4840 or view his website at www.WMitchell.com.

Risk Reversal

Dan S. Kennedy

Many people using my marketing ideas run with this one: "The most thorough or best _____ you've ever had, or your money back." A carpet cleaner: "The most thorough, complete carpet cleaning and cleanest carpets you've ever had, or your money back." A dentist: "The most thorough, gentle cleaning and exam you've ever had, or your money back." A restaurant: "If this isn't the best meal, the freshest home-baked bread, the tastiest Italian sauces, the best service you've ever had in an Italian restaurant, the entire meal is free." Some of my clients and I occasionally guarantee our sales letters. For example: "If you read this entire letter and honestly believe I've wasted your time, I'll donate $50 to any charity of your choice."

These kinds of guarantees are, in a way, arrogant. They are certainly daring. Obviously, if you can't deliver, they are a very bad idea. But if you can deliver, they can be magic, especially in an area where competitors cannot or will not match. For example, a client of mine with a chain of small, independent TV and appliance stores fought off "big box," big name discounters and doubled his business with a penalty. A certain dollar amount was offered as a discount to the customer for every minute they arrived late for a delivery or a service call. For several years he's made this guarantee-with-penalties the focal point of all his newspaper, radio, and TV advertising. He even went so far as to dare any competitor to match his five guarantees in writing, and he promised a $5,000 charity donation if any competitor would. None did.

I am not the only person to ever make hay with this idea. Lee Iaccoca drove skeptical consumers back into Chrysler's showrooms by personally appearing in TV commercials announcing what was then a groundbreaking, unmatched, extraordinary five-year warranty. He simply told consumers: "If you can find any other car manufacturer willing to give you a better guarantee, you ought to buy their car, not mine." This bold move was largely responsible for turning the sick and dying Chrysler company around. By the way, Lee Iaccoca told me personally he not only had no desire to appear in a TV commercial, but was reluctant to do so, worrying that it would be perceived as shameless, egotistical self promotion. He said he did it because he knew it would work. He was right.

I'm always amazed at how eager entrepreneurs and small business owners are to transform their business images to be nameless, faceless, and institutional, when the public clearly and consistently prefers putting its trust in a person.

> Dan S. Kennedy is a direct-marketing consultant. As a highly recognized professional speaker, he addresses over 200,000 people each year, sharing the platform with others such as President George Bush Sr, General Norman Schwarzkopf, Colin Powell, and Zig Ziglar. Dan is the author of How to Make Millions with Your Ideas and *No Rules: 21 Giant Lies about Success*. You can reach Dan at 602-997-7707 or view his website at www.DanKennedy.com.

One of My Biggest Losers

Joseph Sugarman

At the height of my career in direct marketing I had the reputation of being a real winner. It seemed that people thought that everything I touched turned to gold. The trade press was referring to me as a marketing guru, and companies large and small were coming to me with their products.

In reality I was not the big success that everyone held me up to be. I had probably failed more times than most people could imagine. In fact, for every ten ads that I wrote, there was a time when only a few of them became successful. But their success more than made up for the losers—except in a few instances.

You often learn from your mistakes. And if they cost you a bundle, you learn big time. So, I've decided to share with you one of my biggest losers, and explain why I miscalculated so badly.

It was 1975 and my company had done very well over the past several months. We were well entrenched in our new corporate offices and everything was flowing beautifully when a wonderful opportunity came our way. A company in Texas, Corvus Corporation, called to tell us that they had a revolutionary new calculator product called the CheckMaster that did something no other calculator had done before: it remembered what your previous balance was. It had the shape of a checkbook holder, which meant that you could keep your checkbook inside the calculator holder. Instead of having to use a separate calculator and write your check transaction in your checkbook, you could enter your transactions directly into the memory of the unit.

I know that many of you might feel that this is very common and no big deal with all the neat gadgets we have today. But back then, the Check-Master was truly revolutionary.

The president of the company, Charles Sevren, suggested that I come down to Texas as they were willing to give me an exclusive for the product if I was willing to spend a certain amount of advertising dollars promoting it.

So I flew down to Dallas, met with Charles and his staff, and they worked out a great deal for me. I would, upon my return to Chicago, sit down and write an ad for this product. I would then test the ad in the southwestern edition of *The Wall Street Journal*, as I did my other products. If the results were good, I agreed to spend $400,000 in national advertising to sell the CheckMaster.

I created an ad called "Checkbook with a Brain" and tested it with the ad. The ad broke even; just squeaked by with a slight profit. "Hmm," I thought, "If it just broke even, and I roll out in all of the magazines that I've advertised in before, I could possibly do quite well." First, I had an exclusive on the product. No competition. Second, the effect of running the same ad in many different magazines gave a message to the consumer that this was a successful product and that they should join the band-wagon and buy the thing. I realized this from previous experience. And finally, I had this great-looking ad with great copy and, quite frankly, wanted to get my name out there again. Big mistake.

I ran the ad nationally. A few weeks later, as the responses were starting to pour in, I realized that based on previous sales and my current projections, I was about to lose $250,000. The ad was not doing well at all. What I didn't anticipate was that we were entering one of the worst recessions in a long time and consumers were retrenching. They weren't buying on impulse, as they had when I tested the product.

I had a sinking feeling. I had worked for one year to earn $250,000, and now I was watching all that money go down the drain. I had been wrong. First, I hadn't realized that the market conditions could change dramatically. And like any campaign you run in mail order, you can't bet the house on it. Second, your test is an indicator of how much confidence you should have in risking money for a national campaign. And my test told me that I should have proceeded very cautiously and forgotten about the exclusive arrangement that the manufacturer had promised me.

But I was right about one thing. Everybody thought I had a huge success and was making a killing, even my competitors. A business associate con-tacted me and asked "Joe, I've seen tons of ads for the 'checkbook with a brain' and I was kind of, you know, wondering how you were, like, doing."

I didn't want to lie so I answered, "You wouldn't believe how I'm doing!"

To which the associate responded, "No, I believe it. I see your ads all over the place. You seem to get all the neatest products. You really are lucky."

"You should have my luck," was my response.

The Lesson

If somebody gave you a bucket of oysters and told you that there was a valuable pearl in one of the oysters, wouldn't you be inclined to open each one until you found it? So it is in life. We're each handed our own set of talents, skills, and a bucket of oysters. Sometimes that bucket seems huge and it takes a lot of time to find the lucky oyster. But it is always there. The key is persistence. Never give up looking for that valuable pearl. Treat failures as great learning experiences. They help you grow and offer incredible wisdom. And just when you think there is no pearl in the oyster bucket, one will always pop up—and when you least expect it.

> Joseph Sugarman is one of America's leading direct marketing entrepreneurs. He is recognized as one of America's top advertising copywriters. In 1986 he launched BluBlocker sunglasses and pioneered the use of TV infomercials to establish BluBlockers as one of America's top brand names. He has authored five books on subjects that range from personal selling to marketing and motivation. Contact Joseph directly at 702-597-2000 or view his website at www.BluBlocker.com.

When You Hate to Cold Call

Betty Pichon

Marketing can be one of the most daunting business tasks. It takes money, it takes time, and it takes talent and expertise. None of us have all of these at the same time.

Marketing is simply an expression of who you are. You can market positively or negatively, but you cannot not market. Just like you cannot not communicate. Communication can be verbal and non-verbal. Over 58 percent of communication is non-verbal. Thirty-five percent is what people hear in the tone, voice, diction, and accents. That leaves only 7 percent for the actual words you say. In you are not careful, the non-verbal aspects of what you communicate can be more destructive than the verbal. As you are marketing you, be sure to remember that even what you don't say can hurt you!

I hate cold calls. Why? Because no one ever knows who I am. Even if I send a letter a week before telling them what I do and how I do it, when I call they swear they never received the letter, they don't remember, or much worse, they don't care.

To combat this, I had to come up with creative ways of getting people to remember me.

Creative Idea 1

Make sure your mail stands out from the rest.
I send my mailers in a red mailing tube. I use red because it will certainly stand out on a desk of white paper. Inserted into the tube is some sort of promotional item that will make noise, along with my proposal. My proposal is printed on a light parchment paper, with the graphic of a scroll.

Creative Idea 2

Send a gift basket.
Fill the basket with candy and/or crackers, etc., along with your

proposal or advertising and business card. Shrink-wrap the basket with a big bow and have it delivered by messenger.

Creative Idea 3

Use unique postcards.
Postcards are an inexpensive way to get your message out. Each month I send all my clients a postcard printed with a business etiquette tip. At Thanksgiving I send a Thanksgiving postcard printed with the proper etiquette for sending Christmas cards. My clients love these cards and look forward to receiving the next one.

Creative Idea 4

Print your message in different forms.
When I market my business etiquette services to corporations, I print my advertising message on a napkin. I send the napkin in a mailing tube.

Another successful mailer that I have used is a set of clapping hands (the kind you can purchase in a variety store). Along with the hands, I send a message that talks about handshaking and the importance of getting it right. Yes, this is more expensive than most direct mail techniques, but it gets noticed and passed around the office. It gives people something to talk about—me!

Betty Pichon is a trainer and consultant on international customer service, business etiquette, ethics and protocol. She specializes in cross-cultural organizational behavior. Betty can be reached at 480-596-7997 or view her website at www.PichonGroup.com.

Postcards Carry a Big Message

Al Walker

I have noticed how consistently self promotion seems to beget more promotion. Here's an example: every month we mail hundreds of postcards to prospects and customers. I also carry a stack of postcards with me. The one I'm currently carrying has a caricature of me. I have my arms folded and a mike in one hand. Under the picture it simply says, "A Big Man with a Big Message," which has been my speaking byline for over 15 years. I personally mail at least four or five of these a day.

A couple of months ago, I dropped one in the mail to the business editor of our largest newspaper in South Carolina, with a congratulation about something I'd seen in the business section of the paper. On the first Monday of each month the paper publishes a special business magazine, and it always profiles someone the editors feel would be of interest to their readers. I was the profile for the October, 2000 issue, and I'm convinced that postcard helped make that happen.

I believe that good self promotion is simply good marketing. We can learn from the big corporations. If Coke, McDonalds, and General Motors feel they need to constantly advertise their extremely well-known products, shouldn't we do that, too, at least until we become as well known as those three?

> Al Walker is president of Al Walker & Associates, Inc., a firm dedicated to helping businesses and individuals become more productive. Al has conducted over 2,000 training clinics, workshops, and seminars around the world. Past president of the National Speakers Association, Certified Speaking Professional, and a member of the CPAE Speakers Hall of Fame, Al can be reached at 800-255-1982 or view his website at www.AlWalker.com.

Unique Mailers Demand Attention

Craig Campana

When you are a self promoter, you are like a farmer, spreading seed and hoping for a good crop. You water your crop daily by continually sharing your message with everyone in many unique ways. The sunlight (response created by those you market to) germinates the seed and they begin to grow. The result multiplies by word-of-mouth, and your crop really begins to take off.

Make the printed materials you use to promote yourself noteworthy and—by all means—innovative. Leave your mark on your readers with a creative, memorable impression that urges them to take action, pick up the phone, and call to request an appointment or a quote.

When I was active in my video business, Image Associates, I sought out couples planning their wedding. To market myself in a new city where we didn't have much of a network, I chose a creative and innovative approach to capture the attention of our market. I read the society pages of the local newspapers, then sent each couple an invitation to use my services. I designed the invitation to look just like a real wedding invitation. Inside it said:

"Image Associates requests the pleasure of videotaping the wedding and reception of You to Your fiancé on your wedding day and providing a high-quality lasting memory of your special day in video.

With Image Associates, Lights, Camera, Action!

We Guarantee Satisfaction!"

The wording along with a distinctive response card made them react immediately, and I had a 75 percent increase in my wedding videography business using this creative invitation.

Craig Campana is an author, speaker, and networking trainer. He founded the first chapter of Business Network International in Wisconsin. Craig is a contributing author to the book *Masters of Networking*, which has been on the *Wall Street Journal* and *New York Time*'s bestseller list. He is currently authoring a new book titled *Turning Career Adversity Into Power For Success*. Contact Craig at 262-781-7194 or view his website at www.bniwis.com.

Get Immediate Attention with Unique Direct Mail

Debbie Bermont

Have you tried sending out a letter and your company brochure or promotional flyer, hoping to generate a big influx in business or phone activity, and then been disappointed with the dismal results? Do you think most direct mail gets trashed? Have you turned into a direct mail skeptic?

If you answered "yes" to any of these questions, then I want to offer you a renewed sense of hope and confidence. An effective direct mail program *can* generate profitable results for your company.

First, I have to come clean and tell you that a lot of direct mail does get tossed, either because it was sent to the wrong target market, had a lousy offer, or didn't communicate the message in a creative or effective manner. These useless packages are not direct mail; they're junk mail.

If your marketing dollars are limited, then direct mail could easily be a good solution to reaching the *right* target market with your message. The direct mail business is a multi-billion dollar industry, so you know you have a lot of competition for the same person's attention.

Here are a few tips on how you can stand out from the rest of the pack and get your package noticed and read—immediately.

When selecting the correct package format for your program, you need to answer three basic questions:

1. Will the package get opened? Obviously the answer should be YES. If it isn't, then you're wasting your marketing dollars.

2. Will it get past the gatekeeper? Sometimes regular business correspondence never gets past an office administrator. Using unique formats can prevent this problem.

3. What will the reader's reaction be when he or she opens the piece? The important reaction is to get the recipient interested in reading your entire package and then responding to your offer.

Do not consider any package format that does not leave the reader with a warm and fuzzy feeling. If your package is too confusing, has too many involvement devices (i.e., the Publisher's Clearinghouse packages), or irritates the reader (i.e. a package filled with confetti), then you risk turning off the reader right away.

A unique package format can be your best solution to getting the reader's immediate attention. Consider the pile of business-to-business mail you receive everyday in your office. You will probably take notice of any unique package that sticks out from the typical #10 business envelopes or promotional self-mailers. Here are a few ideas that might just do the trick:

1. Make your package lumpy. Stick something in the envelope that gives your envelope three-dimensional appeal. The packaging can include a bubble pack envelope, a box, mailing tube, or even a regular envelope. The key is for the prospect to be *enticed* into finding out what's in the package

   Make sure the lumpy item enclosed ties into the theme of your package. Here are a few examples of items that might be included in a business-to-business package. In most cases you could adapt any of these themes to your own company:

   ▼ A packet of aspirin with the message, "Get rid of your medical expense headaches with the XYZ insurance company."

   ▼ Package of forget-me-not seeds with the message, "Don't forget about spring cleaning. Call XYZ maid service to take care of all your office janitorial needs."

   ▼ A packet of peanuts with the message, "Working with XYZ accounting firm is just peanuts compared to the dollars we can save you in taxes."

   All of these items are relatively inexpensive, but memorable. It is even better if you can print or sticker your name and phone number on the item.

   Please note: When you are considering sending out a lumpy package—especially one that contains a food item—be sure to send a "test package" to yourself first. See how your package gets processed through the postal system and in what shape it will arrive at the recipient's doorstep. It is not advisable to include chocolate, which might melt and damage the rest of the package. Many years ago, one of my clients included packets of mustard and relish in their direct mailers. This proved to be a very messy and embarrassing mistake.

2. There is also an entire line of mailing formats that are creative packages in themselves. They include items in a can, items that make a sound when you open them up, or items that have a self-concealed pen in them. Contact your local premium and advertising specialty company for more ideas. They usually have catalogues filled with fun, attention-getting formats.

3. Greeting cards always get immediate attention. Imagine getting a colored envelope that is hand addressed and looks like a greeting card. It's a welcome relief from the standard business-to-business correspondence. Not only do greeting cards get opened, but many people hold on to greeting cards if they like the picture. Greeting cards can be used as invitations, announcements, birthday cards, customer anniversary reminders, and open house announcements.

4. Postcard mailings are fun, creative and don't need to be opened. They offer a quick way to get your message across. Handwritten postcards are an especially easy and effective way to keep in contact with your prospects and customers. They add a very personal approach to your mailing and help strengthen business relationships.

There are many factors that contribute to the success of a direct mail program, such as having a targeted mailing list, writing compelling copy and having an irresistible offer. But if you don't get your reader's immediate attention, none of the other factors will ever be an issue. Make your next direct mail effort a profitable one with these creative, fun, and attention-getting formats.

Debbie Bermont, president of Source Communications, a marketing consulting firm, has helped businesses nationwide generate immediate results with her simple marketing approach. For more information about the consulting services, speaking programs by Debbie Bermont, business resource tools, and a FREE copy of her e-book, *How to Market Your Business without Spending a Dime!*, go to www.simpleprinciples.com or call 619-291-6951.

Chapter Ten

Self Promotion with Newsletters

What do you want to do?
What do you want to be?
What do you want to have?
Where do you want to go?
Who do you want to go with?
How the hell do you plan to get there?
Write it down. Go do it. Enjoy it. Share it.
It doesn't get much simpler or better than that.

—Lee Iacocca

Shameless Self Promotion Step 10: Publish a Newsletter

Debbie Allen

In the new economy, the customer is king and queen. You've got to ensure that your business model revolves around serving the customer.

One of the best ways to service your customers and promote your business at the same time is with a newsletter. Newsletters educate and inform your customers. At the same time they quietly and shamelessly promote *you*.

You must have a database that you continually build upon. Think about every contact on that list as a gift. Don't ever miss the opportunity to get a prospect's address, phone, and address to add to it. Once you have this information you can be in touch with them on a regular basis.

I'm sure you have heard that your mailing list is "gold." Well, if that is the case, then your email list has to be platinum. By building a complete database of email contacts you will be able to market to your customer base online as well as through the mail. Why would you want to do this? Email is direct mail without stamps! You reach your customer base without spending money on printing and postage—and it's quicker! (Learn more about electronic newsletters from the resources on page 231 and in Tom Antion's confession on page 181.)

Depending on your customer base, decide whether they are best reached with a printed or an electronic newsletter.

Or you may even want to do both. In the 21st century your customers communicate and do business in different ways. You may need to do both to reach a diverse target market.

Shameless Self Promotion and the Art of Motorcycle Maintenance

Dale Irvin

First, I must apologize to you, the reader. When I was asked to contribute to this book, I apparently misunderstood the title. I thought we were supposed to write about "seamless shelf devotion," and it really confused me because I had no idea what that meant. Rather than appear dumb, I did copious amounts of research into the topic of seamless shelf devotion, and found that there is actually a cult on the remote island-nation of Formica that worships the seamless shelf finish bearing their name. During their annual Counter Top Daze (September 31 and 32), they shave their heads and wax their scalps to a glossy sheen while dancing the Hokey Pokey for 24 hours straight. They also have unusual and bizarre intimacy rituals, which I fully intended to write about in this article before I discovered that I was way off base. Instead, here is everything I know about "shameless self promotion."

When I first began in the speaking business I tried to keep in contact with my clients on a regular basis but I soon discovered that frequent long distance phone calls were putting me seriously over budget. What I needed was a cheaper, better, and longer lasting way of letting the people who hired me know that I was still available. I decided that a newsletter would be a good idea. I looked at other speakers' newsletters and decided that rather than providing useful information like they did, I would provide my clients with something they really needed—a good laugh.

I launched "Funny Business" in 1985, and it has continued uninterrupted every month for 15 years. It has grown from a single 8 1/2" x 11" one-sided sheet to a four page, two-color glossy publication with a monthly distribution of 750 potential buyers. I send "Funny Business" via first-class mail and notice a significant increase in phone calls and inquiries soon after it is delivered.

In addition to being a constant reminder to my clients, "Funny Business" has also served as a foundation for stories that appeared in two of my books, *Laughter Doesn't Hurt* and *Dale Irvin Rewrites History.*

Keeping in touch with your clients is an essential part of growing your business, but it is also important to remind them exactly what you do. I make audiences laugh, and I hope I reemphasize that every month when they receive their issue of "Funny Business."

The success of "Funny Business" led to my second shameless self promotional idea. In 1995 I signed up for long distance service with Sprint. Part of their small business incentive promotion at the time was something called Fridays Free, wherein all of the long distance calls made on Fridays were absolutely no charge. What a deal! Unfortunately, after I did the math, I concluded that I would have to be on the phone for 23 hours every Friday to gain any real advantage from this offer. What I needed was a way to benefit from the unlimited free calls that awaited me every Friday.

The answer came to me when I realized that not only were all of my regular business calls free, but all of my outgoing faxes were covered by the same deal. Here was something I could exploit to the hilt. I soon began the distribution of "Dale Irvin's Friday Funnies," a one-page faxed publication that makes fun of the news events of the week. I started sending the Friday funnies to about 100 of my best clients and that number soon mushroomed to include friends, prospects, and subscribers.

The Fridays Free promotion ended in 1998 but I still continue to fax out the "Friday Funnies" to a smaller but profitable list. This idea puts my name and specialty on the desk of every client and bureau with which I do business each and every Friday. Recently I expanded the "Friday Funnies" to appear on my website every week. I hope this will drive more people to the site, and I hope they will buy something while they are there.

These are two simple ideas that get my name and image out to the people most likely to hire me on a regular basis. Whatever forms of shameless self promotion you decide upon, make sure that you do them consistently and that they emphasize the aspect of your business that you want your clients to remember.

> Dale Irvin is a Certified Speaking Professional and a member of the CPAE Speaker Hall of Fame. He has written six books that are not only hysterical to read, but are also reasonably priced. Visit www.daleirvin.com to read excerpts from the books and order on line. If you prefer to talk to a quasi-live person, call 800-951-7321.

Creatively Building a Mailing List

Tom Shay

Several years ago, I noticed that of our 300 charge accounts, approximately half had a zero balance in any given month. I began to wonder why these people failed to find any reason to shop in my business within the past month.

I also knew we were doing nothing special to bring them back again, and their zero balance meant they were not getting a statement from us. One month we decided to trigger the computer system to create a statement for all of the accounts regardless of the balance. On each of the zero balance statements we included a handwritten note, "You owe us nothing. We wish you did. Please come see us."

From this "stunt" we had a number of charge account customers stop into the store. They told us, "I got your message." With this no cost idea, we asked ourselves what we would be willing to pay to get customers to walk in our front door. Initially we did not see a couple of dollars as being too much of an investment to get people to return.

Instead of spending money for traditional advertising, we created a coupon and printed it on colored paper, with eight coupons to a sheet. Again we sent statements to each of the 300 customers, and we included the coupon. Forty percent of the customers returned to redeem their coupons.

With this response, we knew we had a winner, and so we began to experiment with various products to see what customers responded to best. Surprisingly, it was the items that had the lowest cost that people most frequently came in to pick up. As some items required a larger amount of space, the coupon grew to be one third of a page, with additional information about our store printed on the back.

We are not sure when the idea began to grow, but soon we were sending a full sheet of paper, separate from the monthly statement. The paper, which was now our newsletter, had a calendar on the front that told of the store's promotion in the upcoming month. As this feature was added, we decided the newsletter would be sent so that it would arrive in homes around the 24th of the month.

The front contained an article from me, which told of the great things that were going on in our community. In the column I often spoke of other businesses, churches, and residents who had been mentioned in the local newspaper as well as the newsletters of the companies in which they worked. As we found more and more response to the newsletter, we added more advertising from our store and articles about the people who worked in our business.

We placed the newsletters at our check-out counter with a sign inviting customers to take home a copy. Because we knew that there were customers who might not make a point to come in each month to pick up a copy, we changed the sign at the counter about once a quarter with one that said we were not going to be giving out the newsletter at the check out for the next few months. If customers wanted to continue to receive the newsletter, they would need to give us their name and address so we could mail a copy to them. As we saw the list quickly grow, we decided we wanted to see how big the list could be.

We took the information of each person who made a purchase by check, and added it to the mailing list. Any customer who purchased an item that had a warranty, we offered to file their personal information so we could give them a duplicate invoice if their item needed warranty work and they had lost their original receipt.

If we had a contest in the store, we added all the possible names we could find. Within three years, our list of 300 had grown to 2,600. Each name was a person who had shopped in our store, and someone we wanted to invite back to our business.

We then received a bonus that greatly surprised us. A customer who was a real estate sales representative asked for information about placing an ad in the newsletter. She knew there were over 2,000 people receiving the newsletter, and she wanted to use our newsletter to keep her name in front of customers. We quickly came to an agreed upon price and placed her ad in the next issue. We were again surprised when other people and businesses asked about placing ads in the monthly newsletter.

One month as we were totaling the cost of the newsletter, we made a surprising discovery. The newsletter had become a source of revenue. While this did not happen every month, it happened often enough to allow us to further experiment with the newsletter.

We began by asking our vendors to purchase ads in the newsletter. As we continued to offer the monthly free item on the cover, we had vendors who asked to purchase the space and have the monthly free item. We again created the criteria and began to line up monthly sponsors for the coupon item.

Jack Rice, a known retailer, speaker, and columnist, once said, "Never forget a customer, never let a customer forget you." Our monthly newsletter made sure that statement was fulfilled.

> Tom Shay is a professional speaker and a free-lance writer for two dozen retailer oriented trade publications. He authored *EZ Cashflow* and a series of books entitled *100 Profits Plus Ideas for Power Promoting Your Retail Business*, and *100 Profits Plus Ideas for Power Managing Your Retail Business*. Tom can be reached at 888-529-5907 or view his website at www.ProfitsPlus.org.

The Oh-My-Gosh List

Dana Burke

I send out a free newsletter three times a year. It includes tips on marketing and running a small business. Although I do a bit of "back patting," I've learned that I don't have to do much. The quality of the newsletter, its friendly, barefoot feel, and the great resources it offers speak volumes about the type of service I provide. The newsletter is one of the few forms of marketing I do that costs more than a couple dollars. But it's well worth it for the positioning it has helped me achieve in my community.

Besides creating a great newsletter, I made sure I had a great list of people to send it to. This list includes clients, prospects, family members, and local media. It also includes VIPs or what I call my "Oh-My-Gosh List," as in, "oh-my-gosh, I can't believe she reads my newsletter." This list includes big name people, the leaders in my industry on a national or even international level.

A while back I received a call from one of these people, Jane Applegate, the author and nationally syndicated columnist who is an expert on small business. Sure enough, when she told me who she was I said, "Oh my gosh!" She said that she received my newsletter and read it. She didn't know why she got the newsletter as she couldn't remember meeting me (we hadn't met) but that she enjoyed reading it. She wanted to know if it would be okay for her to use an idea I had suggested for her upcoming nationally syndicated column. Boy, would it!

> Dana Burke is the founder of Mind Your Business, providing desktop publishing services and marketing communications for micro businesses and small non-profits. She also publishes "Barefoot Marketing," a free newsletter on marketing your company. Dana has been featured in many publications, including *USA Today, Success* Magazine, and *Business Start Ups* Magazine, and on a variety of websites. Dana can be reached at 414-536-7274.

Chapter Eleven

Shameless Marketing On the Web

*The world is moving so fast these days
that the man who says it can't be done
is generally interrupted by someone doing it.*

—Harry Emerson Fosdick

Shameless Self Promotion Step 11:
Embrace Technology and Market Yourself On the Web

Debbie Allen

Dot-coms are everywhere we look today. While in Venice Beach, California, I saw a man Roller Blading in a Speedo with his website posted on his butt. Now that is about as shameless as it gets—but it sure got my attention!

Back in the early 1990s people who knew a lot about computers and spent a lot of time on them were called "geeks." Today, the "geeks" are the few that don't know about computers, the Internet, and marketing online. We can no longer afford the luxury of not becoming Internet savvy.

There's hope for all of us, no matter how out-of-it you think you are. I confess that just a few short years ago when someone asked what kind of computer I had I said "Beige." I've come a long way since then.

It is great to think that while you are sleeping away, someone on the other side of the world is discovering you on the Internet. And not only discovering you, but wants to do business with you. Just a few months after redesigning my website in order to get it listed higher on search engines and directories, Australia found me. The next thing I knew I was the opening keynote speaker at the Retail Technology 2000 Convention in Melbourne.

Since speaking in Australia, a client requested referrals to other retail speakers. I sent them my associate Tom Shay, then searched the Internet for a retail speaker in Australia. I found John Stanley, checked out his website, and sent him a message so that we could connect.

John emailed me right back. By coincidence he was going to be in Arizona in a couple of weeks. When we met, he confessed that he had downloaded my website just two days before he received my first email. "I printed out a few pages from your site and they were sitting on my desk. I was thinking, 'This Debbie Allen and I may be able to share leads and contacts in one another's country.' Then I got your email."

It's a small world on the Internet, but fishing there is fishing with a big net. You just never know when or where the next marketing "bite" will come from.

Shameless Promotion Internet-Style

Tom Antion

It's a lot easier than it used to be to be a shameless self promoter. In the bad old days you had to go to networking meetings and press the flesh with a bunch of people who were more interested in getting business than giving it. Or you had to hang out at professional associations and hope someone would throw you a crumb.

Not anymore. The Internet has changed all that for savvy self promoters. Now you can promote yourself at night while sitting in front of your computer wearing ragged shorts and a three-day growth. (Women, substitute no makeup and fuzzy slippers.)

Here's the three-pronged Internet promotion attack I teach in my Butt Camp seminars.

Prong One: Build a Great Website

...and learn how to do it yourself. I don't mean you have to create the whole thing yourself, just how to update it. This was the best investment in time and money that I made throughout my entire career.

Get a professional to create the main page and the basic look of the site. It has been my experience that many designers know how to design a gorgeous-looking site, but you need to add the content that will help you sell. So, purchase some simple software and take about 15 minutes to become familiar with it. When you are, you can add page after page after page of solid content to your site yourself. You'll save yourself a ton of frustration overall.

Once you have the site up and running, spend part of your time promoting it and part of your time adding new pages. I teach the big target theory. The more content-rich pages, carefully constructed to attract search engines, you have, the more traffic and business you'll enjoy.

It's up to you to learn the website elements, strategies, and psychology that get people to pull out their credit cards. If you are in the dark about good website marketing, you won't get much out of your site.

Get some good training in this area. There are many books on the subject, and new ones are coming out all the time. This is a rapidly changing field and a fascinating new way to do business.

Prong Two: Build a Targeted Email List

This is where the money is. When you build an email list of targeted people that have asked for information from you, you can cut the costs associated with traditional marketing methods—design, printing, postage, labor, agency fees, airtime, etc. Your risk goes down to zero, and your return on investment skyrockets.

You won't be alone either. Companies large and small are gathering email addresses for the same reason: cheap and quick marketing. You can hardly find a website that doesn't entice you to "log in," "sign our guest book," "get free tips via email," or have some other strategy to get your email address. This is all responsible, "opt in" email marketing. It is not "spam," which is sending promotional email to any email address you can beg, borrow, steal, or buy.

Here's the implied bargain you are striking with the people that get your emails. You send them information that saves them time, makes them money, gives them the information they want, or in some way benefits them. In return, they agree to stay on your list so that you can market to them.

You have to do a little experimenting with your target market to find the right balance of information, marketing, and frequency. Send too many self promotional pieces and other ads and people unsubscribe. Send anything too often and they'll leave you even quicker. On the other hand, send lots of great information with no marketing content and you'll be wasting your time because you haven't given them a chance to buy.

Keep in mind that a small, targeted list will make more money than a big, general list. With a targeted list you can define the wants and needs of the people on the list and create products and services that they will want to buy.

Getting people to sign up isn't all that hard. Your great website (Prong One) attracts people you would never have found in any other way. Directories and limited direct mail can get them on the list at minimum cost. Do whatever legitimate thing you have to do to get that email address, and then your promotion is for free from then on.

Prong Three: Product Development

You may have noticed that we have a one-two punch going so far. Your great website pulls in new people, and your electronic direct mail markets back to them. But what are you marketing?

You've got to have a product base. You may already have a line of products, but as your customer base grows, you can survey them to find out about needs that you can fulfill. When you find out about what your target audience wants, then you can either adapt your products or create new ones to fill these niches. Your own customers will tell you what they want.

In addition to the traditional hard goods that most companies sell, many businesses have knowledge that people would buy if they had the chance. Informational products in the form of books, tapes, CDs, audio- and videotapes, and downloadable products are all very high profit, low risk add-on ventures. These informational products actually make it much easier to sell your traditional or main product line. The whole idea is to distribute good and helpful information to earn the trust of your market.

Once you've earned their trust by exposing them to your knowledge, your customers will become much more comfortable spending money with you. This is especially true on the Internet. Most people are still apprehensive about buying online. If they take the plunge with you and have a good experience, they are very likely to stick with you and buy everything you put out.

So, if you're interested in shamelessly marketing yourself electronically, learn how to create and update a kick-butt website, build a targeted email list you can promote to for free, and develop products or giveaways that showcase your knowledge. Do these three things and don't be ashamed when you make bigger bank deposits.

> Tom Antion is the author of the Wake 'Em Up Video Professional Speaking System and creator of the infamous Butt Camp Seminars, where you learn to make more sitting on your rear end than you ever did out working for a living. View Tom's website at www.Antion.com or by email at Tom@Antion.com.

Saved by the Internet

Daniel Harrison

I started a small pool service company in 1980, and worked out of the basement of my house. In 1983 we opened a service company of a pool store, and then we became one of the first companies in the area to get into the new thing, selling hot tub spas. We did so well that we soon opened up one of the first "all hot tub spa" stores in our area, Long Island Hot Tubs. Throughout the 1980s we sold hundreds of spas and built elaborate spa rooms, greenhouses, and decks. In fact, our business was so successful that we received numerous awards within our industry.

Then the recession of 1990 hit. Times were tough and thousands of people lost their jobs. Of course, luxury items like pools and spas were the first thing to be cut from people's budgets. We went from selling over 150 spas a year, to only 30 in 1991, and we had no choice but to close our store and file bankruptcy. It was Long Island Hot Tubs darkest hour!

Luckily we still had the pool and spa service companies, but also a very large problem. When we had the store most of our income came from the sale of spas and spa rooms; we thought of the repair and service as a necessary evil. Selling spa chemicals and accessories was merely a convenience to our customers. Now we had to support ourselves and make up for all the money we lost on the store with this side business. We had to totally rethink our sales strategy fast.

We had a mailing list of over 2,000 spa owners, and we did not want to lose their now valuable chemical and spa service business. We figured that if they could no longer come to our store, we had to bring the store to them! So we started publishing the *Long Island Hot Tub Newsletter* (now called *Hot Tub Life*).

The first few issues were a little rough, but almost immediately customers told us that they loved the newsletter and that they got a lot of information from it. They also told us that it was much easier for them to order their supplies over the phone than come to our store. We knew that we were on to something good.

Within the next few years our pool and spa repair service business almost quadrupled. We had to hire more service people and office help to keep up with the calls. We received more than 200 calls a day in peak season, and we had to figure out a way to handle the volume more efficiently. We quickly realized that in a phone order type of business, phone time equals money, and the quicker we could process each order, the more customers we could serve each day. So we invested about $30,000 in a custom network computer system that allowed us to process repair service and product orders more quickly. Going from computer illiterate to completely networked took some getting used to, but we all survived.

In the mid-nineties we started to hear about the Internet. We were immediately interested because we could finally expand our spa chemical and accessory mail order business nationwide. We had thought about it before, but national advertising was just too expensive. On the Internet we could do it for much less cost.

We started to learn all we could about the Internet and how to build a website. We worked for over six months to plan, develop, program, and launch our first 150-page site, "The Virtual Pool & Spa Store." Within a

year we were dealing with pool and spa owners from all over the country and had increased our mailing list to 22,000 people! We could just see it getting better and better every month.

It is important to note that this was way before the term "e-commerce" had even been coined. Not only were we a forerunner in the pool and spa industry, but we were ahead of most other businesses. Truly, we were in the right place at the right time with the right idea!

With Internet sales increasing at a comfortable rate, we were able to establish both larger offices and a bigger storage and shipping facility. We decided that we should rename our website to the more generic *Poolandspa.com*. Then we separated the content portion of our site from the online shopping area, which allowed us to sell advertising on the content website and not conflict with the shopping area. This site is now the world's largest pool and spa website, with over 2000 pages of articles, information, pictures, and products.

Our business has been featured on numerous TV and radio shows along with books and magazines on e-commerce. Because of that, we have often been called an "overnight success." We hate that saying. Although it is meant as a compliment, it does not acknowledge that this company's journey has been a long one, with many ups and downs and years of hard work.

Walk Before You Run

If you do not have a website, carefully consider your end goal. Be realistic about what the Internet can and cannot do for your company. Do not contact a web design company until you have decided where you want your company to go and how you want to get there. If you go to a web design consultant without definite plans, you will end up with a site that is disappointing or overkill for your business—and with an astronomical price tag as well.

Start small and build up. It took six years but that's what we did. Go for quality, not quantity. A consumer is going to be far more impressed with five to ten well-thought-out and properly designed pages than 50 to 100 sloppy, amateurish ones. Remember, your website is going to be compared to all the big sites out there. Compare your site to others—both within your industry and out—and make sure yours holds up.

The great thing about the Internet is that it offers so many different possibilities. The trick is to find the niche that fits your business plan the best. Then make a professional looking website that reflects your business.

> Daniel Harrison worked his way through college as a professional magician and a pool cleaner. He started Paramount Pools, which developed into The Virtual Pool & Spa Store. Poolandspa.com is now the largest pool and spa website in the world. Call 800-876-7647 or view this extensive website at www.PoolsandSpa.com.

You Have to Give in Order to Receive

Wayne Perkins

Have you heard the expression, "The quickest way to reach your goals is to help others reach their goals"? I use this as my Internet marketing plan. My mission in business and life is to help others achieve their mission in life. I do this by supporting them with lots of free information about Internet marketing strategies that have worked for me.

I have two areas of expertise. I am a hypnotist who writes books on how to achieve success through hypnosis. I publish them in both print and electronic form. In addition, I consult with other authors on how to develop a successful electronic book presence on the Web.

Everyone Wants to Be at the Top of the Heap

Those who run the top websites spend a great deal of time and money to remain at the top. Everyone wants to be there, but only a few can hold down those top positions.

To keep your website consistently in the top search engine standings you must add to and change its content often—sometimes as often as once or twice a day. In addition, your site should offer an e-zine or electronic newsletter delivered via email daily, weekly, or monthly.

Search for the Big Guys on the Internet

In order to find the top websites that may be interested in information on hypnosis, I search broader topics, such as "health" and "mental health." For my books on e-book marketing I search on topics such as "Internet marketing" and "e-commerce."

Even though there are hundreds of search engines and thousands of directories, I begin my search on Yahoo. Yahoo is a directory that is difficult for websites to get into. It is even more difficult for a website to maintain a high ranking. Therefore, it is there that I am going to find the best websites.

Once I made the top of the Yahoo heap under "hypnotism" my web traffic more than doubled. It has stayed that way for the past three years. Therefore, if you get your website to rise to the top of Yahoo, you will be much more highly visited than through other search engines and directories.

Once I search under the two major categories that fit my topic, I send email to the webmasters at the sites I have found, along with my article, newsletter, or a sample chapter of one of my books. Most webmasters jump at the opportunity for the content that allows them to maintain their high rankings on search engines. In return, I ask them to post my bio and add a link to my site. In this way I help the webmaster offer more content on their site and/or e-zine, and I get exposure. It's a win-win for everyone.

By helping the webmaster add content and the newsletter editor offer new articles, you will drive targeted traffic to your website. This not only translates into a top-ranking website; it will help you fulfill your online marketing goals.

> Wayne Perkins is the bestselling author of *A Cheap and Easy Guide to Self-Publishing E-Books*. To learn how to write and sell your first e-book, contact Wayne at 602-647-4280 or view his tele-classes and website at www.WaynePerkins.net.

Golf Guru Goes for the Gold

Michael Anthony

At the 1984 Olympics in Los Angeles, I helped Kevin Winter make the US weightlifting team. Before the 1988 Olympics, two-time yachting world champion Lynne Jewel asked me to mentally prepare her and her team-mate Allison Jolly to win a gold medal. They not only made the US Olympic yachting team, but they dominated their competition and brought back the gold.

After my Olympic successes, I decided to target this mental training program specifically for golfers. Not being a golfer myself, I studied their emotional reactions. The key to my mental training program is being aware of why and how to control your negative emotions, which play havoc with performance.

Armed with the facts that trigger negative emotions for golfers, I took my mental training program to the golf mecca, Palm Springs. There, with a simple bet I shamelessly enticed over half the head pros to pay handsomely for a two-hour personal consultation. "If you don't feel my program will improve your golf after our session, don't pay me." I never lost a bet, and the head pros happily wrote out their checks.

After putting my mental training into a book, *The Mental Keys to Improve Your Golf,* I launched a website to market it. In addition, I added a free weekly mental golf tip in an electronic newsletter format. This information helped prospective customers understand my mental training program and how it would benefit them.

Today, as a special bonus for purchasing my book, via email I answer any questions customers might have about improving their mental game. When asked why I offer so many valuable services over the Internet for free, I always say, "I love helping others improve. It's nice to know that my mental training program works, even over the Internet and at all levels in golf."

My program has helped Olympians win gold medals. It's just a matter of time before I have helped professional golfers win on tour. Then *The Mental Keys to Improve Your Golf* will become my gold medal.

> Michael Anthony is the creator and author of *The Mental Keys to Improve Your Golf.* You may contact Michael directly at 925-820-4824 or view his website to learn more about his services at www.MentalKeys.com.

Sales Horror Stories

Dan Seidman

I created a unique persona for myself that promotes my business of reporting on sales people who have crashed and burned. The product I created is a short, funny story of people's worst selling experiences. To that, I add my expert analysis of what went wrong, so that others might avoid the mistakes of their colleagues.

My logo is a chalk outline of a dead guy (like those you see at crime scenes). This is very unusual and gets lots of comments.

My signature file in my emails is key to marketing my website. It is intriguing enough that most people I contact visit the site before calling me. Many of the phone calls I receive begin with laughter as people say "I love your site, my favorite story is…" Laughter is a huge rapport generator and sets the conversation on a great foundation.

Here's my short, but effective email signature:

Dan Seidman, the War Correspondent of Selling http://www.SalesAutopsy.com
Sales Horror Story Library, read 'em and weep (or laugh)

Seven Steps to Attacking the Market

1. My best marketing play has been to offer my stories as syndicated content for websites and print publications. During the first few months that I contacted editors, response was so high that my total readership was around five million. I'm currently marketing to 30 different associations, web portals, and trade publications about carrying my content.

2. I belong to important moderated newsgroups (check out John Audette's highly successful family of newsgroups at www.audettemedia.com. By offering insights to others in my exact target market, I've gained recognition and traffic.

3. When you read something that impresses you, contact the author. I've nurtured many relationships with authors over the years and they pay off in many ways. I've maintained a relationship with guerrilla marketing guru Jay Conrad Levinson for about five years by doing this. The pay off? He's agreed to write the introduction for my book of sales horror stories. This is obviously a big credibility builder.

4. Create a newsletter that helps you stay in touch with your target market. Make it brief. Contact other newsletter editors in your target market and ask them to review or mention your new publication. Run your own contest to get readers interacting with you. The SalesAutopysy.com contest awards an inexpensive watch with the dead guy logo for any story that makes the newsletter. The watch cost me about $3.25 each and are an unusual branding tool (and toy).

5. Write a funny or fascinating press release. Mine is titled "Sales Horror Story Website Reveals Sins of the Salespeople." Spend some time each week sending the release to appropriate editors on the Web. A good way to find them is to go to the library or local book superstore and browse the magazines. Find the web address of the magazine and go there to get the email of the editor.

6. Two incredible resources that have highly benefited my marketing plan:

Associations Unlimited

This is a listing of associations on every topic you can imagine. Search their CD-ROM for organizations with which you should partner or who might write to members about you. It's very expensive ($2,500), so I suggest going to the library to access it. Ask the reference librarian for assistance with the software.

Gebbie All-In-One Media Directory

A comprehensive resource that lists radio, TV stations, daily and weekly newspapers, trade and consumer magazines, news syndicates, and more. Use this resource to get to the right people in your target market. You'll be amazed at who is out there that you never knew about. View this site at www.Gebbie.com.

7. Subscribe to these free, indispensable online newsletters.

Dr. Ralph Wilson (www.wilsonweb.com) has over 100,000 archived articles related to doing business online. He compiles the best of the big publishers and shares them with readers.

Larry Chase Web Digest For Marketers (www.wdfm.com). Larry is the author of *Essential Business Tactics for the Net.*

Dan Seidman has been involved in high-impact sales and marketing for businesses for over 20 years. Dan is the president of SalesAutopsy.com, where he edits and produces a nationally syndicated column of stories entitled "Sales Autopsy: A Post-Mortem of Your Sales That Died." This site includes a collection of the worst and most embarrassing sales experiences from entrepreneurs and sales professionals. A free subscription to Dan's newsletter of selling disasters is available at www.SalesAutopsy.com. Dan is available for some hilarious speaking engagements that include his great, gruesome selling disasters. You can reach Dan directly at 847-798-8515.

> *One of the reasons people stop learning is that they become less and less willing to risk failure.*
>
> —John W. Gardner

Chapter Twelve

Lights, Camera, Action — You're ON!

> *If you can image it, you can achieve it.*
> *If you can dream it, you can become it.*
>
> —William Arthur Ward

Shameless Self Promotion Step 12: Apply For and Win Awards

Debbie Allen

People skills are the key to making it big with the media. You may have the best products and/or services in the world, but if you can't communicate effectively, then your voice will not be heard. Think about it: Hollywood is 100 percent personality driven. Shamelessly marketing yourself to the media is like becoming a star in Hollywood. The most famous people in the world do not sit back and wait for the media to notice them. No, they run out in front of them and yell, "Look at me! I've got a talent to share with the world." After the media starts to notice them, they attract even more media attention—sometimes to the point of frustration. I don't know about you, but I wouldn't mind holding back the media from noticing my business. Bring it on!

The best way I have gotten media attention is by being nominated for and winning business awards. Once you have won an award you can use it to your advantage over and over again.

Here's how it worked for me. It started when a couple of my shameless marketing friends nominated me for awards. I reciprocated and nominated them as well. One especially shameless marketer was my friend Rochelle Balch (see her confession on page 118), a dynamic lady who was winning award after award as she built her business. Rochelle coached me on how to create an award-winning portfolio. Each award application required slightly different information, but I was ready with my detailed portfolio, which included my biography, major achievements, and details on how I overcame obstacles in my business. When opportunities arose I was ready to meet deadlines.

This went on for a couple of years as I was nominated for award after award. Even though I was contacting the media and getting lots of press with my nominations and my story of success, I still was not winning. (Kind of like always a bridesmaid, but never a bride.) I was ready to give up! I told Rochelle, "You win all the awards because your business is more newsworthy and mine is not as unique." She replied, "Deb, you don't realize what you have accomplished. When more than 50 percent of all businesses fail, you have had huge growth despite your obstacles of little money to invest and no experience in your chosen fields of retail and professional speaking. Keep applying, I know you are going to win because you deserve it." Rochelle's support kept me motivated.

Within six months I received a call from John Davies, Executive Vice President of Mass Mutual Insurance, "The Blue Chip Company." John said that he had read my story in the Phoenix newspaper and had been inspired. He kept the article in a file for over a year. Today he was calling to nominate me for an award that their company founded, The Blue Chip Enterprise Award, which is sponsored by the U.S. Chamber of Commerce and *National Business Magazine*. Finally, I had won! I was the recipient of that award for the state of Arizona in 1997.

What does winning an award do for you? Boost your ego? Well, it might, but in business there is no room for a big ego. What it will do is give you the opportunity to promote over and over again and get free advertising for your business. Is it worth all the effort? You bet! Now this is where shameless self promotion comes into play: You must work it to the max, sending press releases and contacting the media as often as you can.

One major airline took shameless self promotion to another level. They created their very own award. They actually went down to the trophy store and bought the largest trophy they could find. Then they invited the media to a big party and presented themselves with a business service award that they had created. Not surprisingly, this same airline has won this prestigious (or so it seems) award for the past five years. Now I don't recommend this, but I must admit that it did work. (Just a little too shameless for my taste.) I suggest doing it the right way: apply over and over until you win.

Here's how to apply:

1. Obtain applications for awards and complete them in detail. Don't rush. Take your time and get it right.

2. Profile your business. It is important to respond as completely as possible. This will help to establish a relative benchmark for evaluating your success.

3. Describe the major challenges that have threatened your business or opportunities that you created. For example, this may include challenges such as new competition that developed, loss of major clients, or a downturn in your industry.

4. Give your solution and the results. Describe the resources and results that you used to overcome the problems. Award programs often look for insights into the management of your company's resources in personnel, quality assurance, marketing, community, and financial areas.

Seven Tips for Winning Awards and Self Promoting Your Business

1. Seek out opportunities to get nominated. Opportunities are everywhere. Your local organizations, Chamber of Commerce, Better Business Bureau, and the media are just a few places to look.

2. Show your professional best. The applications for awards are usually lengthy and detailed. It takes some hard work on your part to collect the data and put it together in a portfolio, but it will be well worth it. To win, your entry must stand out because of its attention to detail and professionalism.

3. Follow the rules on the application. Read all entries thoroughly and prepare the documents in accordance with the

contest rules. If you do not understand something on the forms, call and ask for clarification.

4. Look at your entry from another prospective. Keep in mind that judging for most of these types of competitions is done on a matrix-type scale; each item requested will have a point value.

5. Get your entry in well before the deadline. Make it a priority to get the paperwork completed and mailed on time. Once you have an award portfolio and files saved in your computer, the process goes quicker. You can then easily go into your file, make adjustments and additions, and print out.

6. Contact the media. Whether you win or get a nomination, this is your chance to work it for maximum exposure. Write a press release emphasizing the award, and send it to local newspapers, magazines, and radio and TV stations.

7. Display your award proudly. Create a "wall of fame" that attracts attention in your office or sales area. In this competitive environment, nothing sets you apart or enhances your company more that winning an award. The media exposure you receive will be far more effective than any advertising ever will.

Keep applying, and best of luck!

Woman of the Year
Patricia Fripp

Shameless self promotion is part of my nature. I'm always looking for the next opportunity. With the scent of shameless self promotion in the air and the vision of myself on a billboard, I couldn't resist the opportunity that came my way back in the early 1990s. At that time many charitable organizations were experiencing greater-than-usual cash flow concern. They needed to raise cash quickly, and most of them planned to do this with the support of the community, which created value for all involved.

One such organization was the San Francisco Leukemia Society, which was going to benefit from an event sponsored by Hastings (a successful retail clothing company). The individual who raised the most money for the leukemia society in a five-week period was to be named Hastings Man or Woman of the Year.

It was my goal, as a participant in this event, to raise $30,000. I knew that the prior year, the entire contest had raised that amount. I met the goal, and I was named Woman of the Year! I felt great about making a valuable contribution, and at the same time I was increasing my own community exposure. I had my photograph taken in a Hastings suit and was featured on ten billboards throughout the community. The billboards were donated by a major billboard company.

Taking a Great Opportunity to the Next Level

The mayor proclaimed a "Patricia Fripp Day" in San Francisco. When the first billboard was unveiled, I hosted a party to celebrate. Hastings provided champagne and helium balloons, while I supplied t-shirts and buttons for those attending. Then, taking the opportunity to still another level, my speaking colleagues volunteered to write songs celebrating my contributions. "There's No Billboard, Like Fripp's Billboard" was sung to the music of "There's No Business, Like Show Business." Another was a rap tune, "The Fripp Rap" or "Gimme Your Money." Both were performed at the event.

I had the event video taped, hired a Mother Theresa look-alike to bless the billboard and keep it graffiti free, and enlisted an Elvis impersonator to make a surprise appearance. By inviting all my contributors and friends, we were able to create a big stir on the street corner, attracting the attention of passing motorists and weekend shoppers.

Then Hastings and I rented a booth together at a Chamber of Commerce business showcase and brought a monitor to show the video of the billboard party. By splitting the expenses, we both benefited from my personality draw at the booth.

At Christmas Hastings organized and paid for a catered party in my honor at one of their store locations. I gave a speech, "How to Win in a Recession." The event and seminar drew a large crowd from the community. I invited friends, associates, and contributors, including my Fripp Singers and Rappers. We gave gift bags, which included my audio cassette pack, specialty advertising giveaways, an expensive writing pen, along with other premiums and bonuses provided by Hastings, to all attendees.

I had accomplished what I set out to do and, in the process, created additional value for those who chose to participate. Synergy prevailed; the leukemia society received donations far beyond their expectations, Hastings got the exposure they were looking for—and more, and I received tens of thousand of dollars worth of promotional exposure.

Look for your opportunities and make the most of them. Keep shameless self promotion in your arsenal. You can surely do more than you might first believe. Keep this in mind the next time you get invited to participate in a community event, and make your shameless self promotion a win-win for all.

> Starting out as a hairstylist from England, Patricia Fripp is now a successful entrepreneur, magazine columnist, and a "speakers' speaker." Patricia has won every award and designation given by National Speakers Association, and served as its first woman president. She is the author of *Make It, So You Don't Have to Fake It!* and *Get What You Want!* Patricia can be contacted at 800-634-3035 or view her website at www.Fripp.com.

Much More than Your 15 Minutes of Fame

Marilyn Ross

Want more than 15 minutes of fame? The old axiom, "Success breeds success" is so true. The media likes to climb on a moving bandwagon. Consequently the more exposure you get, the more exposure you'll get. And you can see to it that this happens by recycling your publicity. Reprints allow you to impress. Inform. Motivate. Educate. Persuade.

Recycle any print coverage that appears. It doesn't matter that the original publication's circulation base is smaller than your neighborhood. What counts is what you do with it! Although an amateur will be satisfied with what they get, a pro will milk it for all it's worth to stay in the limelight. That shameless marketing pro will double and triple the bang for their publicity buck.

I have a specific strategy for recycling my publicity. Because I belong to many associations that publish newsletters that include "member news," I have all those newsletter editors on a database. When something happens, I write a short generic news release and customize the beginning to match their format. Then I mail, fax, or email it immediately. Publicity is sort of like a boomerang: you have to throw it before it can come back. Consider being incestuous: do a press release about your press release!

Get copies of everything written or broadcast about your company. It's important to keep track of your clips. If you're doing a local campaign, you can probably track down any articles with an observant eye, a few phone calls, and perhaps a Web search. For a broader PR campaign, use a clipping service to capture what is said about you.

Newspaper and magazine article are often missed the first time around. Yet articles make people think your company is important and unique because the publication chose to write about you. Obtaining reprints provides a way for you to make sure existing and potential clients, customers, suppliers, bankers, stockholders, etc., get a look.

Most magazines offer reprinting service for somewhere between 75 cents and $1 apiece for a four-color reprint. Have them add your logo, address, phone number, and website for added impact. Also consider matting and framing a copy to hang in your reception area, office, or shop. If you own a retail establishment, put copies on the counter with a "Take One" sign. By doing so, you turn unbiased editorial material into a marketing piece that delivers real impact.

These print pieces solidify your credibility. They provide an ideal, low-key reason to get in front of prospects and should be used as a mailing for anyone you're trying to woo. Send copies to current clients or customers as well. Use them as enclosures in virtually everything you mail. Use quotes from the pieces in your marketing and sales materials. Mention any articles in your company newsletter. Obtain permission to put them up on your website. And when soliciting additional publicity, include what has already been done. This helps establish your newsworthiness.

> Marilyn Ross is the award-winning author of the new book, *Shameless Marketing for Brazen Hussies: 307 Awesome Money-Making Strategies for Savvy Entrepreneurs.* Ross dipped her toe into entrepreneurial waters at age nine and has run a multitude of successful companies ever since. A marketing consultant and professional speaker, Marilyn can be reached at 719-395-2459 or view her website at www.brazenhussiesnetwork.com.

Magic Phrases to Use with the Media and What to Avoid

Joan Stewart

"How can I help you?"

Those are the five magic words you should ask media person you come in contact with. As a former newspaper editor, I can assure you that almost no one asks that question. Instead, people who want stories written about them—even authors and publishers—mistakenly beg, plead, grovel, cajole, and make pests out of themselves. To get in the media's good graces, here are more magic phrases you can use if you have a reporter on the phone, or you are writing a pitch letter to an editor.

"I can provide other sources for your story."

Reporters love this because they don't have to work hard tracking down other people for multiple-source stories. Sometimes this is the only way you will be mentioned in a story.

"When is your deadline?"

This shows you are respectful of their time. It also gives you a good idea of how quickly you might have to provide the information the reporter is seeking.

"Please call on me for other story ideas on this topic."

Reporters and editors will welcome this, and they will probably take you up on your offer.

"What other information are you looking for?"

If you can lead the reporter in the right direction, you'll earn valuable brownie points.

"I have written material which I can provide."

Reporters often appreciate having information in writing so they can refer to it later. It also helps improve accuracy.

"I can provide graphic illustrations you might want to consider to accompany your story."

Print media like things such as maps, pie charts, illustrations and other graphics. You will save them valuable time if you can provide these.

"Would you like me to send a media kit so you can review it before the interview?"

This is a thoughtful gesture. It helps reporters prepare.

"Would you like me to provide a list of questions you can ask me?"

Ask this question only of broadcast media, such as radio talk show hosts. Never ask print media if they need questions or they will be insulted.

Here are other tips for staying off the media's enemies list:

▼ After an interview, don't ask the reporter if you can read the story before it goes into the paper. The answer will be no—at least from any reputable publication.

▼ Don't come back after the interview and ask the reporter to remove certain sensitive quotes and other information you gave on the record. It may result in bad feelings, distrust, and eventually, end what could have been a good relationship.

▼ Don't give an editor or reporter the idea that they are getting an exclusive, when in fact you already talked to a reporter at another publication who was interested in your story.

▼ Don't agree to be interviewed, then cancel because you change your mind. The reporter will never call you again.

Joan Stewart is a speaker, trainer, consultant, and expert in media relations and employee recruitment/retention. Joan can be reached at 262-284-7451 or view her website to sign up for the free weekly e-zine "The Publicity Hound's Tips of the Week." In addition, receive a free copy of "89 Reasons to Send a News Release" by auto-responder at www.publicityhound.com.

Applause! Applause!

Susan Brooks

It's showtime! Anytime, every time, you can get the attention of the media, you've won the lottery. As I was growing Cookies from Home, my advertising budget was not only very small, but it was the first thing to be eliminated if the priority was to keep the lights on. And, even today, no matter how big my advertising budget has grown, I could always spend more.

Regular television ads, non-seasonal radio ads are beyond my reach, even today. In my early years I was forced to be creative to get media attention. Today I have to be even more creative to keep their attention. But, I will tell you this, there is nothing—I repeat, nothing—more valuable, more immediate, and more image building than free press.

I had a definite advantage over most…I had our mouth-watering, baked-from-scratch, homemade cookies. Every promotion, every PR release, every media contact I ever met received a big box of our award-winning cookies.

Cookies open a lot of doors; cookies make people feel good; cookies helped me to make new friends…media friends who liked my product and the human interest element of my story. My job, which became my mission, was to think of as many creative ways as I could to keep Cookies from Home in the news.

My Shameless Media Story: An Edible Art Show

In support of the Shakespeare Theater Fest, for the Scottsdale Arizona Center of the Arts, I had the brilliant idea to contact the largest and most reputable resorts to display some Shakespearean/Elizabethan food sculptures. This would create a happening, an event that would attract crowds of sophisticated, fun-loving, food-loving people (cookie lovers, everyone) and lots of press. Each food sculpture would be auctioned off to the highest bidder and the monies would be donated to underprivileged school children, who would then be able to buy tickets to see Shakespeare on stage, probably for the first time.

What did this do for me and my company? First, it put me in touch with the movers and shakers in the community and in marketing, as well as head chefs at the most prominent resorts in my city. These are people who would not only use my product, but could refer me to others as well. Also, by association, even though I was a very small, entrepreneurial company at the time, I appeared a lot larger when connected in this way. Their high-quality reputations helped me to develop and reinforce our own image as well.

I knew the profiles of the people who would attend this event would be of the ideal potential customer for Cookies from Home. Our product is a high-end, high-quality, high-impact gift idea. The right audience just needed to know about us.

Next, because this was my idea and I chaired this part of the festival, I was also the media contact. I met media people and stayed connected to them before, during, and long after the actual event. Their interest and, more likely, curiosity kept them involved and provided great coverage, which was a win/win for everyone involved: the general public, the Scottsdale Arizona Center for the Arts, the participants, and of course, the under-privileged school children.

Great media coverage brought thousands of people/customers to the art center. A cream cheese bust of Queen Elizabeth, chocolate curls for hair; an Elizabethan castle made from cakes and elaborately colored icings; a seven-foot tall Lady MacBeth made from different kinds of cookies, with walnuts for fingernails and coconut flakes for hair; all this and more raised money for a community cause and provided exposure for the Scottsdale Arizona Center for the Arts and the participating resorts. These were the ingredients for a huge success!

You can do this. Yes, it was lots of hard work, from sharing the initial vision to enrolling others then making it a reality, but it worked!

Your goal is to get yourself and/or your company known with or without an advertising budget. Your exposure, your involvement in a community and/or business event becomes a marketing tool, which can lead to additional editorial coverage. This will build your brand recognition with the consumers.

Start by asking a few questions so that the strategy that you create will bring the results you want:

1. Who are my customers? What are their ages? What do they like to do? Where do they go? What is their financial profile? Use your answers to create a profile customer and go where they are! Let your customers see you in a different mode than what is usually expected.

2. How can I stand out? Once you know who your customer is and where you can find them, make sure that you and your company stands out from all the rest. This is your chance to be discovered; use this opportunity to the max!

3. How can I create follow up? If you give something away, you can usually get something in return. Create a database for future follow-up and connection. Stay present. Don't let customers, prospects, or contacts forget you.

4. How can I serve? You don't need to push, you don't need to try so hard. Come from the desire to serve, to help, to fill a need. A quality product with quality and genuine service is always appreciated in the marketplace.

So take the leap into the showtime arena. Life is theater so why not play a winning part? You have everything to gain, and nothing to lose. And, you know what? Your enthusiasm will be contagious! Go for it!

Susan Brooks is cofounder and president of Arizona-based Cookies from Home. In addition, Susan is a professional speaker and columnist. As a customer service enthusiast, she addresses key customer service issues. You can contact Susan at 480-994-1918 or by email at ToBServed@aol.com.

Recycle This

Charlie Hawkins

In the early 1990s, my company produced a high school assembly program about recycling, with the ultimate objective of generating publicity for its sponsor, a large plastics manufacturer. "Recycle This!" used popular music and live actors to deliver its message. It ultimately toured 100 cities in the United States.

In attempting to generate media coverage, we had a PR agency send out a slick press kit that explained what the program was all about and why it was different than the typical high school assembly. With this approach, we were able to attract some attention, but well below what we wanted. Then we realized that the slick materials were the problem, a truly shameless approach that didn't work.

We decided on a backdoor way to get the publicity. Once the cast and crew arrived in a city, we sent the show's production manager, in road dress—jeans, sweatshirt, etc.—to television stations and newspaper offices. She contacted the person responsible for environmental issues and told them that she was with a traveling group of concerned people who were committed to the environment. She further explained that they had developed a show about recycling, which was a movement just getting underway at the time. The sponsor was not mentioned initially.

This approach was the winner. In city after city, the media were attracted to this grass roots program. In almost every city we visited, local TV stations ran something on the evening news, and newspaper coverage was heavy. Inevitably, the media reps asked how the program was funded. Then, and only then, did we mention the name of the plastics company. Seen in this light, the sponsor's name almost always made it into the stories. Later, the show was covered by CNN *Headline News*, ABC, and *USA Today*. In 1991 it was recognized as one of the outstanding public relations programs of the year.

Charlie Hawkins, MBA, works with organizations that want to encourage a climate of fun, creativity, and risk-taking and with people who want to express themselves more persuasively. He has been closely associated with some of the most innovative products and marketing concepts of our time, including Bounty Towels, Mennen Skin Bracer, and Dr Pepper. Today, as a nationally recognized expert in the areas of creativity and communications, he shares his insights in keynotes, workshops, and retreats. Charlie can be reached at 520-204-2511 or by email at seahawk@sedona.net.

The Luckiest Unlucky Man Alive

Bill Goss

When I was just nine years old, I plunged my head into a sink full of water, hoping to get the wet-head look of Elvis Presley. My head wedged between the two faucets as the water poured in. My screams dissipated into gurgling noises as my face became immersed in water. I thought for sure I was going to drown.

My head was too big and the basin too small. There was simply no way I could get my hands around my face to unplug the lifesaving stopper and drain the water. Neither could I move my face down far enough to pull it out with my teeth.

I survived by ripping out two hunks of scalp and denting the faucet handles. It was the first of 30 near-death experiences that I survived over the next 30 years. The list goes on and on, as I evolved from a long-haired 18-year-old garbage man in New Jersey to a sound-barrier breaking Navy pilot flying around the world. With personal experiences that range from being in a cave-in while dynamiting 5000' underground in an Arizona copper mine to being the pilot of a Navy spy plane during a major crash on a runway in Spain in 1984.

Then, if you think things couldn't get unluckier, in 1991 I stopped my car on the Interstate to remove a large box of garbage from the middle of the highway that was going to cause an accident. As I stood in the median, an out-of-control car going 50 mph struck the left side of my body. I flew 45 feet through the air and had a wild out-of-body experience, but broke no bones, and was flying Navy airplanes a few weeks later. Lucky or unlucky?

But the most life-threatening experience occurred the day after I broke the sound barrier in a Navy F-18 Hornet off the coast of Florida in 1994. A small bump on my left ear, one inch from my brain, was diagnosed as very deep malignant melanoma tumor, a deadly cancer caused by the sun. I had a one percent chance of survival. I was told I would be dead in six months. During 12 hours of cancer surgery, the left side of my face was removed—a lot like in the movie FACE-OFF. Doctors then took out my jugular vein, my shoulder muscle, my salivary glands, 200 lymph nodes, and most of my left ear.

Thankfully—and luckily—I've been cancer-free now for seven years. A brilliant plastic surgeon reconstructed my left ear from material harvested from one of my ribs and a piece of my left groin. My left ear looks great—but you can imagine what happens to it now when my wife kisses me goodnight!

What do all these lucky and unlucky misfortune have to do with self promotion? Make the most with what you've got! My unique story has inspired much of the publicity I have received. My autobiography, *The Luckiest Unlucky Man Alive*, has received lengthy and favorable reviews in major newspapers across the world.

Since the book was published, I have also been a featured guest on hundreds of popular radio and television shows around the world including The Discovery Channel's *Animal Planet*, *EXTRA*, *Maury Povich*, *Sally Jesse Raphael*, ABC, NBC, CBS, PBS, Ted Nugent in Detroit, and Rick Dees in Los Angeles. I even worked with actress Demi Moore as an extra in the movie *GI Jane*. In addition, I'm the only man alive to have successfully survived a live interview on both *The Howard Stern Show* and *The 700 Club*. That's not only adversity—that's diversity!

> Bill Goss is a "totally unique speaker." His upbeat, inspiring, and sometimes hilarious message on how to overcome great challenges and adversity appeals to an extremely wide-ranging audience. Bill has spoken to audiences around the world and with other celebrity speakers such as Bob Dole. Now living in Florida, former Navy pilot Bill Goss can be contacted at 904-278-8900 or you can view his website at either www.GetLuckyNow.com or www.BillGoss.com.

My Time to Shine

Millie Szerman

As a publicist whose first line of work is promoting other people's stuff, a surprising turn of events led me to shine the spotlight on myself. Not once in years of operating my business from home had I ever contemplated writing a book about working from home. Up until the 1990s, working from home wasn't necessarily something you publicized. Fast-tracking success up the corporate ladder was the hallmark of that time, and most people and corporations didn't know how to classify home-based entrepreneurs. You might say I was home-based before home-based was cool.

By the mid-nineties, America was warming up to the concept of working from home and *Money Magazine* included me in a story on how millions of Americans were earning six figure incomes at home. Ahh…the spark that torched a blaze…the beginning of my life as a shameless self promoter.

Sure, I could have done my interview, posed for a few quick shots in the home office, working at the computer wearing bunny slippers…but (and most people who know me will agree) that's just not my style. And so, in my shameless self promoting way, I turned the magazine photographer's casual compliment about my spa-like bathroom into a cover photo that illustrated the idyllic work-at-home lifestyle. There was cover girl me, soaking in a tub full of bubbles, chatting on a red cordless phone with my handy day planner and a glass of wine nearby. When the March 1996 issue of *Money* rolled off the presses, it became the magazine's top-selling issue. The last time I checked, it was STILL the magazine's No. 1 bestselling newsstand issue ever!

The thousands of calls and hundreds of hours I spent fielding inquiries I received from my initial plunge into self promotion led me to write and self-publish my first book, *A View from the Tub: An Inspiring and Practical Guide to Working at Home.* (How great it was to have the cover shot already done—the same one as on *Money Magazine!*) As luck would have it, I've been self promoting ever since.

When Millie Szerman appeared on the front cover of *Money Magazine* wearing nothing but bubbles, a red telephone, and a smile, the business world sat up and took notice. Szerman runs her public relations and marketing consulting firm, New Directions, from her home office. She has appeared on numerous television and radio programs nationwide. Millie can be reached by phone at 310-798-8990 or through Stairwell Press at www.StairwellPress.com.

> *Whenever you are to do a thing,*
> *if it can never be known but to yourself,*
> *ask yourself how you would act*
> *if all the world was looking at you,*
> *and act accordingly.*
>
> —Thomas Jefferson

Chapter Thirteen

Fame, Fortune, and Your Name in Print

> *The saddest words of tongue or pen*
> *are these four words "it might have been."*
>
> —Oliver Wendell Holmes

Shameless Self Promotion Step 13: Write a Book

Debbie Allen

Quit saying, "Someday I'm going to write a book." If you are a truly shameless self promoter—or strive to be one—you need to write a book! This is where the truly shameless shine. Having the title of "author" gives you a great deal of credibility.

A few years after I wrote my first book, the excitement of being an author had worn off. I decided it was time to write book number two. I worked on the second book, *See Through Your Customers' Eyes*, for three years. (Don't rush out to buy it, since that one has not yet been completed.) Then a funny thing happened. I started listening to what other authors had told me for years; "Don't write a book until it's burning passionately inside of you." Those words made me shift focus from my current book project to a new idea.

At the National Speakers Convention in the summer of 2000, the idea for *Confessions of Shameless Self Promoters*™ hit me. The passion flamed. I couldn't wait to get on my computer and put the idea into printed words. In fact, it burned so brightly that I shelved the other book and went full steam ahead with *Confessions*. That passion helped me to complete this book in just six months. It can be done when you have a winning concept and a strong commitment to getting it down.

Wendy Keller, a book agent, says that the key to getting your book written is "Butt in chair!" You just have to keep at it everyday and put hours and hours in that chair to make it happen. Some of the best books and winning concepts did not take years and years to write. They came in the form of information, passion, and a commitment to share your thoughts and words with the world. So if you have that book idea burning inside of you, sit down and get writing.

When you are done writing, the real work begins. Get out of that chair and market that book. It doesn't matter how great your book is, if you don't market it, the world will never know about it. The book marketing experts in this chapter will show you the way.

Five Promotions a Day

John Kremer

After I wrote *1,001 Ways to Market Your Books*, people kept coming up to me to thank me for writing a wonderful book. They would then make excuses for why they hadn't followed up on any of my suggestions. Well, don't even think about coming up with your own excuses now. I'm going to give you the rule that forbids excuses. I call it "the rule of five." The rule says that all it takes is five promotions a day. Really, that's all it takes. Mail a letter. Send out a news release. Phone someone. Take an editor to lunch. Contact the media. It need not take much time—15 to 20 minutes is enough—but it can make a world of difference on how well your book sells.

Essential Points for Pursuing Media Exposure

1. 75 to 80 percent of all news is planted. That means, most of the news you read in newspapers and magazines has come out of news releases sent to the media by businesses, associations, government offices, and other organizations or individuals with something interesting to say.

2. If you can provide real news for the media, they will be glad to feature your book. That's why you should keep refining your news hooks until you find one that really meets a need. Don't send out a press release announcing any book until you can show that the book provides at least one benefit for potential readers—whether entertainment, information, instruction, or enlightenment.

3. Publicity begets more publicity. Once you get the ball rolling, it will often go on by itself. Local news features are picked up by the wire services and spread across the country. Local radio and TV shows can lead to bookings on network shows. One or two features in the major review media, and soon every newspaper in the country is calling to ask for a review copy (or simply reprinting the review from one of the major sources).

4. If at first you don't succeed, try, try again. Persistence, above all, is the key to success in generating favorable publicity for your book. Believe in your book, keep on plugging away, and the reviews will come.

No more excuses! If your book hasn't sold, there is only one reason (provided the book has any merit at all). And that reason is: You're just plain lazy. If you spend just twenty minutes a day, every day on every book you publish, you will generate an incredible momentum for your book.

There is no reason why any book should die after six weeks in the marketplace. Books, like diamonds, are forever—provided you are willing to put a little elbow grease behind their promotion and you use those ten minutes a day wisely.

Now get off your rear end and start doing your ten minutes a day right now. Don't wait. I mean it. Don't wait.

John Kremer is the author of a number of books on publishing and marketing. His bestselling *1,001 Ways to Market Your Books* has made him the nation's top book marketing guru. John's marketing tools, seminars, and books have helped thousands of authors and publishers. Contact John at 641-472-6130 or view his website www.bookmarket.com.

Bright Ideas Turn Around Author's Reviews

Dan Poynter

Editor's note: Dan Poynter's The Self Publishing Manual was the victim of cyber-terrorism. I got Dan to confess his story.

A very negative one-star review was posted at Amazon.com and went so far as to recommend another book instead. Then, the perps went back and said they found the first "review" useful—25 times! There was also a three-star, unsigned review that appeared to be from a disgruntled typesetter. Anonymous attacks by those who refuse to sign their work are cyber-terrorism.

Dan called a friend for advice. The friend told Dan that he tracks his Amazon sales very carefully. He received some negative reviews by the author of a competing book and his sales dropped precipitously. Dan got scared.

Dan contacted Amazon.com about unsigned negative reviews that are obviously designed to promote another book. Amazon's position is that these comments are legitimate customer assessments. (They probably feel that negative review-wars build site traffic.)

There were 21 reviews (one heck of a lot) of *The Self-Publishing Manual* on the Amazon.com site; 19 had five stars. The two negative reviews dropped the overall rating to 4.5 stars.

Dan called one the authors of the other referenced book, told her the nasty one-star review of his book referenced her and made her look bad. He suggested she contact Amazon.com to have the review pulled. She apparently knew about the review. She thought over Dan's suggestion and emailed him that she would not take action.

So, Dan went to Plan B.

First, he came out with a new edition of his book. He printed out the online listing page and edited it for Amazon.com. He asked them to make the normal reference at the end of the offending reviews; "This review refers to an earlier edition."

To further build credibility for the new edition, Dan sent Amazon.com a lot of new promotional material. He sent the table of contents, back covers

220

copy, testimonials, and a free read of two to four pages from EACH chapter.

Next, he went on the Pub-Forum Listserv and asked for advice. Dozens of publishers came to his rescue with sympathy and advice. Five posted reviews immediately at Amazon.com, which was enough to move the nasty review off the first page. About 25 publishers asked for review copies and promised to write reviews. Dan sent books to them immediately.

Then another idea struck: Dan wrote a (five-star) review of the offending book and posted it at Amazon.com. Between his call to the author and this review he hoped to telegraph that he would not slug it out in the gutter. There is a higher road. (Of course, he signed the review "Dan Poynter, author of *The Self-Publishing Manual*. DanPoynter@ParaPublishing.com.")

Dan sincerely believes there are a lot of good books on self-publishing. He supports them. Almost all of them have a testimonial from Dan on the cover, or he wrote the foreword. People new to publishing need all the books, tapes, courses, and other education they can get. Buying a few more resources is cheaper than making a mistake.

Learning from this experience, Dan wrote 21 more Amazon.com reviews for books on writing, publishing, self-publishing, and book promotion. Each one is labeled "Reviewer: Dan Poynter, *Author, The Self-Publishing Manual*." Now his name and the title of his book are near the top of each listing page.

Sometimes the best way to fight cyber-terrorism is to take the high road and lead by example.

> Dan Poynter has coached thousands of writers and publishers to the next level in book promotion. He is a frequent speaker, successful publisher, and renowned book publishing consultant. His seminars have been featured on CNN, his books have been pictured in *The Wall Street Journal,* and his story has been told in *US News & World Report.* The author of 113 books and more than 500 magazine articles, he recently published the twelfth revised edition of *The Self-Publishing Manual.* Learn more about Dan at www.ParaPublishing.com.

If at first you don't succeed, skydiving is not for you.
—Dan Poynter

Fit to Cook

Denise Hamilton and Chantal Jakel

We are two nurses, Denise Hamilton and Chantal Jakel, and we left our secure, no shift work, weekends-off jobs to become entrepreneurs. Parents and friends thought we were foolish, some said that it made even less sense when they heard that we left our stable nursing positions to write a cookbook. But wait, maybe it did make sense. We "saw a need and filled it," to use a standard business cliché. Furthermore, we truly believed in our product.

"Actually, I haven't written it yet. I'm doing the promotional tour first, to see if being an author is really the right career move for me!"

From our work with cancer patients who also suffered from unhealthy eating-related diseases such as obesity, high blood pressure, heart disease and diabetes, we knew that most people do not eat a sufficiently healthy diet. Because of the time constraints of our hectic jobs, we were unable to spend sufficient time with patients to help them with their dietary concerns. That's when the light bulbs came on. What these patients needed and wanted was a cookbook that would be like having a nurse in the kitchen with them everyday. It would outline a month of menus, and include an exercise program. The cookbook is called *Fit to Cook: Why "Waist" Time in the Kitchen?*

People who used the cookbook began talking about how easy and delicious the recipes were. The local media became interested, and the bookstores began to call. In less than two years, we sold 240,000 copies of our book. How did we do it? We learned to market and do publicity—constantly. We learned that "you have to be in somebody's face every day," as Denise always says. That is certainly not something we learned in nursing, where the patients came to us and we were behind-the-scenes support staff. Now we have to be the front runners, the media personalities, and the autograph signers.

We began with local newspapers and magazines, local television and radio stations, and local book-signing sessions. We hired a media training coach before progressing to regional media. Then we produced our own video to capture the interest of the national media gurus.

Once we were comfortable with public appearances, we turned our attention to marketing. Then we accomplished a major coup. A large pharmaceutical company purchased 187,000 copies of our book, followed shortly after by the sale of 45,000 books to a major women's healthcare organization. Our reputation was established as the providers of an easy-to-follow, healthy lifestyle plan.

> Denise Hamilton and Chantal Jakel are former nurses who quit their jobs and risked the "family farm" to write *Fit to Cook: Why "Waist" Time in the Kitchen?* This book is their contribution to preventive medicine and exercise. There is no other cookbook like it! The book is available at www.fittocook.com or by calling 888-678-4044.

An Authentic Hawaiian Luau

Patricia Fry

One thing I've learned about promotion and marketing is that if you have something that is of value to a segment of the population and if you put in the time and effort, you will hit upon the magic recipe for selling quantities of your product and/or your services. If the goods or service is not what folks are looking for, it will take a little longer to convince them they should have it.

I wrote a book on the fascinating true story of my experiences working with a hypnotherapist who specialized in past-life regression therapy. It is a book everyone on a spiritual path would surely want to read, I thought. The other book I wrote was a fun little guide to presenting a Hawaiian luau on the mainland. I don't think I could have chosen two topics any more distant than these, which made promotion extremely difficult to manage. It took me a few months to realize that I was doing a disservice to both books by applying the scattershot method.

When I evaluated sales at the end of three months, I discovered that I was actually making money on the luau book, while the metaphysical book was costing me money to promote. So I decided to concentrate my efforts where flow had been established. That's when I became a shameful marketer. One of the wildest things I did was to put on a full-blown luau, complete with a roasted, whole pig for a group of 100 strangers. This came about when a newspaper reporter, responding to one of my many press releases, asked if he could photograph a luau. I asked him to give me a few days to think about it. The next day a friend called for an entirely different reason. In the course of the conversation, she mentioned that she was in charge of putting on a seventieth birthday party for a friend, and she was stuck for a theme. I blurted out, "How about a luau?" She liked the idea and the race was on. I had less than three weeks to coordinate an authentic Hawaiian luau, but the event was a success from all angles.

One thing I've learned as a promoter/marketer is to never say, "No." Sometimes you will be asked to make a presentation, give a workshop, or maybe teach an aspect of your topic or your business. It's easy to slide down into your comfort zone and say, "I don't have the time." I see my colleagues do this all the time. I've learned to say "Yes" to such invitations, and then I figure out a way to do it.

> Patricia Fry has been writing for 27 years, and has contributed hundreds of articles to magazines, including *Entrepreneur*, *Writer's Digest*, *The Toastmaster*, *Cats*, and *Christian Parenting Today*. Patricia has authored ten books, and has been writing full-time for over 12 years, which takes tons of nerve and constant shameless promotion. You can view her writing at www.Matilijapress.com.

Polite Persistence

Jacqueline Marcell

When I wrote my book *Elder Rage or Take My Father...Please!: How To Survive Caring For Aging Parents*, I really didn't have a clue about publishing. I had just lived through an incredible nine month experience with my elderly parents, and I felt beyond passionate about getting the word out to others about how to manage their challenging elderly loved ones. I had never written anything but a postcard and did not have a degree in any aspect of medicine (does photography or cinematography count?) but I was sure that I'd find a publisher for my "Elder War and Peace" (with a twist) masterpiece right away. What I did have was many years as a sales and marketing executive in the television business, university-level teaching experience, and lots of naive *chutzpa*.

By looking through *Literary Market Place* and *Writer's Market*, and lying on the floor of Barnes & Noble in the health/aging section, I located 130 publishers who had ever published anything about eldercare. I called them all up and left a riveting voice-mail pitch on as many editors' phones as I could. I timed each company's voice mail and left as much detail as possible before being cut off. Well...sixty responded with, "Yes, send it right away." (Even without an agent!)

I gleefully sent off my labor-of-love manuscript and then unhappily received fifty-seven rejection notices, but...there were also three offers. I was thrilled out of my mind until I got the contracts. As a new, unknown author I was offered a few hundred dollars up front, a very minimal royalty, a requirement to publish my next book with them (yeah, like I'm ever gonna go through this again), and a requirement to give them some rights to the movie as they were sure a book deal would produce a movie offer. I tried to negotiate (they thought for sure I'd cave in), they wouldn't budge so I finally said, "Uhmm, no thanks—I'll do it myself."

I poured over several books on self-publishing, took some classes, networked like crazy with self-published authors, and decided that since I was a nobody, the only way my book would be taken seriously would be to have numerous celebrity endorsements. That would get my foot in the door and then the book would have to measure up.

226

I found out that SAG (Screen Actor's Guild) would give me agents' phone numbers for three celebrities at a time, and you'd better have your names ready because they are very busy. For authors, I sent the manuscript to their publishers. The reference librarians at the local library got to know me real well, helping me research how to find some of these people.

I put together a riveting cover letter, my bio, a can't-put-it-down five-page synopsis, and sample quotes of what I was looking for. I faxed, emailed, or mailed this package to hundreds. Then I called to follow up only to hear: "Sorry, we didn't get it…Please re-send it…That person doesn't work here anymore…You need to talk to the manager…No, we don't handle that… You need to talk to the publicist…Didn't anyone tell you he never endorses books?…We get hundreds of these requests a month…I'm sure she'd have no interest in a book like that." It was never bada-boom…bada-bing.

Polite persistence turned out to be the key. Re-send, re-leave messages, re-email and re-fax until their offices knew my name pretty well. "Hi, just me, Jacqueline Marcell again," until I finally got their attention. Those who were interested in the topic asked to see a full galley. Then…wait, wait, wait for them to read it, evaluate it, and respond. One celebrity's assistant told me, after seven months of polite phone calls, "He said that if you called one more time, he'd give it to you because of your pleasant persistence." I was always very polite (okay, I begged a little), but I was careful never to be obnoxious or annoying.

I realized I had really hit a chord with my topic when, eight months later, I had 40 impressive quotes from: Steve Allen, Ed Asner, Jacqueline Bisset, John Bradshaw, Phyllis Diller, Hugh Downs, Leeza Gibbons, Dr. John Gray, Mark Victor Hansen, Art Linkletter, Ed McMahon, Regis Philbin, Dr. Dean Edell, Senator John D. Rockefeller IV, Duke University Center for Aging and The Johns Hopkins Memory Clinic, to name a few…but I don't really like to name drop.

I was so elated when the quotes started to come in. Did you hear me screaming when I got Hugh Downs? One celebrity called and said he loved it but was ill and asked if I'd mind taking his quote over the phone. Uh, not at all! To save them time and energy, I always sent several suggested quotes, geared just to them. If they were too busy, all they had to do was pick one and make it their own. One celebrity said, "I like them all. Slap my name on any one of them and put me in there—I love what you've done."

I was surprised that celebrities were so willing to help, but then I realized that they hadn't always been celebrities and other people surely helped them along their way. When they see something worthy of their name and their help, many are willing to lend a hand.

Of course, I sent everyone an autographed copy of the finished book with a note of my everlasting gratitude. I believe that because of their valuable endorsements I've been able to become an advocate for eldercare awareness and reform much faster than I would have otherwise. I am now a sought-after speaker at conventions and on radio and television, helping thousands of adult children and spouses cope and get the answers they are searching for. I always have to laugh because the very first question any interviewer asks is, "How in the world did you get all these incredible endorsements?" I always say, "I hit a chord with an issue they care about, had a good product, and then I begged—ever so politely."

> A former professional photographer/cinematographer, university professor, and television executive, Jacqueline Marcell gave up her life for nearly a year until she succeeded in turning her extremely difficult elderly father around. She credits the Alzheimer's Association for managing his complex brain chemistry and then she did behavior modification on him and changed life-long behavior patterns. Contact Jacqueline at 949-975-1012 or visit her website at www.ElderRage.com.

The worth of a book
is what you can carry away from it.

—James Bryce

13 Steps To Shamelessly Successful Self Promotion
By Debbie Allen

Step #1: Develop a Strong Belief System.

Step #2: Keep a Positive Attitude and Contagious Enthusiasm.

Step #3: Develop Gutsy Goals that Make You Stretch.

Step #4: Seek Out and Act Upon Opportunities.

Step #5: Stay Active in Your Community by Networking and Volunteering.

Step #6: Take Your Expertise to Another Level.

Step #7: Build a Strongly Connected Group of Strategic Alliances.

Step #8: Break the Mold, Then Shamelessly Promote Your Uniqueness.

Step #9: Get Out in Front of Your Target Audience On a Regular Basis and Don't Ever Stop Reminding Them About Your Business.

Step #10: Publish a Newsletter.

Step #11: Embrace Technology and Market Yourself On the Web.

Step #12: Apply For and Win Awards.

Step #13: Write a Book.

References

Special Event Resources

Chase's Calendar of Events
NTC Contemporary Publishing Group, Inc.
4255 West Touhy Avenue
Lincolnwood, IL 60646-1975
Phone: (847)-679-5500; Fax: (847) 679-6388

Celebrate Today
Open Horizons
c/o John Kremer
P O Box 205
Fairfield, IA 52556-0205
Phone: (800) 796-6130; Fax: (641) 472-1560
Email: jfkremer@kdsi.net

Postcard & Flyer Resources

Modern Postcards (customized with your photo/message)
800-959-8365; www.ModernPostcards.com

1-800-Postcards (customized with your photo/message)
800-Postcard; www.1800Postcards.com

Web Cards (postcards to market your website)
800-352-2333; www.Web-cards.com

Color for Real Estate (offers free catalog of unique mailing ideas)
800-221-1220; www.ColorForRealEstate.com

Retail Edge (unique promotional mailers)
800-777-2445; www.Retail-Edge.com

Tu-Vets (four-color flyers)
800-894-8977; www.Tu-Vets.com

Public Speaking/Leadership Skills

Toastmasters International
800-993-7732
website: www.Toastmasters.org

Recommended Reading

Authorship

The Self-Publishing Manual, How to Write, Print, and Sell Your Own Book by Dan Poynter (Para Publishing)

1001 Ways to Market Your Books by John Kremer (Open Horizons)

Jump Start Your Book Sales by Marilyn & Tom Ross (Communication Creativity)

Direct Marketing and Newsletters

Marketing Secrets of a Mail Order Maverick by Joseph Sugarman (DelStar Books)

2,239 Tested Secrets for Direct Marketing Success by Denny Hatch & Don Jackson (NTC Business Books)

Quick and Easy Newsletters by Elaine Floyd (Newsletter Resources)

Internet Marketing

Self Promotion Online by Ilise Benun (North Light Books)

Striking It Rich.com by Jaclyn Easton (CommerceNet Press)

Click, The Ultimate Guide To Electronic Marketing CD by Tom Antion (Anchor Publishing)

101 Ways to Market Your Business, Products and Services on the Internet by Raleigh Pinskey (Brass Ring Publishing)

Marketing and Self Promotion

Secrets of P-O-W-E-R Marketing by Peter Urs Bender and George Torok (Stoddart)

Guerrilla Marketing Excellence by Jay Conrad Levinson (Houghton Mifflin Co.)

Shameless Marketing for Brazen Hussies by Marilyn Ross (Communication Creativity)

101 Ways to Promote Yourself by Raleigh Pinskey (Avon Books)

232

Networking and Referrals

How to Work a Room by Susan RoAne (Harper Collins Quill)

The Secrets of Savvy Networking by Susan RoAne (Warner Books)

Masters of Networking by Ivan R. Misner, PhD & Don Morgan M.A. (Bard Press)

Pushing the Envelope All the Way to the Top by Harvey Mackay (Ballantine Books)

Endless Referrals by Bob Burg (McGraw-Hill)

Public and Professional Speaking

Speak and Grow Rich by Dottie & Lilly Walters (Prentice Hall)

What to Say When You're Dying on the Platform by Lilly Walters (McGraw-Hill, Inc.)

Make 'Em Laugh! How to Use Humor in Presentations by Tom Antion (Anchor Publishing)

Involving Your Audience by Karen Lawson (Allyn & Bacon)

Inspire Any Audience by Tony Jeary (Trade Life Books)

Resources for Newsletters:

Do-it-yourself electronic newsletter:

> *The Handbook of Ezine Publishing*
> www.E-zine.com

Do-it-yourself printed newsletter:

> *Quick and Easy Newsletters* by Elaine Floyd
> published by Writer's Digest Books
> www.NewsLetterinfo.com

Professionally printed newsletter production and design service:

> Put It In Writing
> 877-588-1212
> www.Put-It-In-Writing.com

Retail

Up Against the Wal-Marts by Don Taylor & Jeanne Smalling Archer (American Management Association)

100 Profits+Plus Ideas for Power Promoting Your Retail Business Series by Tom Shay (Profits Plus)

1,001 Ideas to Create Retail Excitement by Edgar A. Falk (Prentice Hall)

Trade Secrets of Retail Stars by Debbie Allen (Success Showcase Publishing)

No Thanks, I'm Just Looking by Harry Friedman (Kendall Hunt Publishing Company)

Retail Business Kit for Dummies by Rick Segal (Hungry Minds Publishing)

What Mother Never Told Ya About Retail by T.J. Reid (Retail Resources)

Sales & Motivation

Gung Ho! Turn on the People in Any Organization by Ken Blanchard (William Morrow & Company)

Fish! Catch the energy and release the potential by Stepen C. Ludin, Ph.d., Harry Paul and John Christensen (Hyperion Books)

How to Sell Yourself by Joe Girard (www.JoeGirard.com)

Outrageous! Unforgettable Service —Guilt-Free Selling by T. Scott Gross (American Management Association)

The Diversity Advantage by Lenora Billings-Harris (Oakhill Press)

How To Close Every Sale by Joe Girard (Warner Books)

Success

No Rules: 21 Giant Lies about Success and How to Make It Happen Now by Dan S. Kennedy (A Plume Book)

The Acorn Principal by Jim Cathcart (St. Martin Press)

Mastering Your Way to the Top by Joe Girard (Warner Books)

Multiple Streams of Income by Robert G. Allen (John Wiley & Sons, Inc.)

Seven Habits of Highly Effective People by Steven Covey (Simon & Schuster)

Getting Everything You Can Out of All You've Got by Jay Abraham (Truman Talley Books / St. Martin's Press)

Money Is Easy: How to Increase Prosperity, Attract Riches, Experience Abundance and Have More Money by Larry Winget (Win Publications)

Laugh and Grow Rich by Darren LaCroix and Rick Segal (Specific House Publishing)

Personal Success and Lifestyle

Chicken Soup for the Soul™ series by Mark Victor Hansen and Jack Canfield (Health Communications, Inc.)

It Only Takes a Minute to Change Your Life by Willie Jolley (St. Martin Press)

1001 Ways to Be Romantic by Gregory J.P. Godek (Casablanca Press, Inc.™)

How to Really Love the One You Are With by Larry James (Career Assurance Press)

Hit Any Key to Energize Your Life by Gail Howerton (Quick Study Press)

It's Not What Happens to You, It's What You Do About It by W Mitchell (Phoenix Press)

The Luckiest Unlucky Man In the World by Bill Goss (Lucky Press)

Real Moments by Barbara DeAngelis, Ph.D. (Delacorte Press)

Men, Women, and Relationships by John Gray (Beyond Words Publishing)

Index